COMPLETE GUIDE TO MAKING

Wire Jewelry

Printed in the United States of America.

11 10 09 08 07   1 2 3 4 5

Publisher's Cataloging-in-Publication Data
(Prepared by The Donohue Group, Inc.)

Complete guide to making wire jewelry.

  p. : ill. (chiefly col.) ; cm.

  The projects in this book were featured in Art Jewelry magazine.
  Includes index.
  ISBN: 978-0-87116-254-0

1. Jewelry making--Handbooks, manuals, etc. 2. Wire jewelry--Handbooks, manuals, etc.

TT212 .C66 2007
745.594/2

Contents

Introduction

Welcome to the art of making wire jewelry. You'll find yourself in excellent company here. More and more jewelry makers are turning to wire as a way to express creativity through making beautiful jewelry in a variety of styles from simple to intricate, classic to contemporary. In this volume you'll find step-by-step projects by a variety of artists whose techniques and knowledge have graced the pages of *Art Jewelry* magazine. The contributors and editors who share their expertise in these pages come from many different backgrounds – metalsmiths, hobbyists, artists, and jewelry enthusiasts all have a voice. Some have advanced professional degrees, while others are entirely self-taught, but they all have taken the time to explore this wonderful medium and to share their creativity and techniques with readers. We're happy to present that knowledge here.

Jewelry artists are drawn to wire for many reasons. Wire allows jewelry makers to create beautiful pieces without all the "heavy equipment" of metalwork. Then there's the beauty of the material itself. The gleam of silver and the brilliance of gold can be easily bought in a form that one can shape into coils, textiles, and frames. The projects in this book are appropriate for jewelry makers of any level. Some projects require only a few basic tools, such as pliers and cutters, while more advanced projects require more tools, and even specific designated work areas.

We've made an effort to create a guide that's easy to use, even for beginners. In each chapter the projects progress from easier to more difficult, allowing you to build on your skills as you progress through the book. Each section focuses on a different approach to working with wire, concentrating on a specific range of techniques and concepts. You'll find each section filled with a variety of ideas and tips. A photo-illustrated guide to the basics of wire, essential tools, and fundamental techniques covers the vital information you need to get started. And if you encounter an unfamiliar term or technique, or need help finding a particular tool or supply, our easy-to-use reference section is there to help. All you need to do is grab some wire and get started.

Basics

WIRE

Buying wire is fairly easy, but it's best to know a little about your choices before you buy. Try to buy the most appropriate material for your project. You'll find that some wires work better than others for different purposes. Understanding the materials, shapes, and gauges of wire can make wireworking that much more successful.

Wire is available in a wide range of materials. Gold and silver are the most traditional choices, but wire also is available in brass, copper, and niobium, among other options. When you are first starting out, you may want to try copper or inexpensive craft wire to learn techniques such as coiling or making hooks. These wires are easy to manipulate and much less expensive than silver or gold.

Silver

There are four common options for silver wire: fine silver, sterling silver, Argentium silver, and German silver. Of these, fine silver is the purest, composed almost entirely of silver. However, fine silver is a fairly soft material, so it is not ideal for certain jewelry elements, such as clasps, closures, or hooks, which take a lot of

stress. If certain elements don't require a lot of strength, such as a head pin for hanging a single bead, use fine silver. It will stay white and lustrous without much polishing since it oxidizes at a slow rate. It also doesn't have to be pickled after heating if used without flux.

Sterling silver and Argentium silver are perfect for most jewelry-making applications, since they have been alloyed with other metals for additional strength. Sterling silver has long been the material of choice for jewelry makers, since it is strong and malleable. Sterling silver is 92.5% fine silver with 7.5% copper and other metals – thus the .925 stamp on sterling. The drawback to sterling is that this small copper content makes it oxidize at a faster rate than fine silver, so it tends to tarnish quickly. Argentium silver is an alloy that substitutes a higher content of germanium to avoid the tarnishing problem while retaining the strength of the metal. Argentium is considered a great techno-logical advancement in silver, having the best qualities of sterling without its oxidation rate, but Argentium is a bit stiffer than sterling to work with.

German silver wire is frequently found in beading stores and craft shops. This wire is formed by layering sterling silver over a copper core. The copper makes the wire very malleable and easy to use, but if you have exposed wire ends (as on wrapped loops), or if you need to hammer your wire, the copper core of the wire will show. For that reason, many jewelry makers avoid German silver wire.

Gold

Gold wire is available in different karat weights, tempers (see p. 6), and even colors. 24k gold is pure gold, but very soft to work with, while 14k gold is a $^7/_{12}$-gold alloy. For those of you who love the warm, silken appearance of gold but want to keep the costs of your jewelry-making endeavors affordable, gold-filled wire is an economical choice. It's a fraction of the cost of 14k-gold wire. Contrary to its name, gold-filled wire is actually gold overlay. A thin layer of 24k gold is heat- and pressure-bonded to a brass core. The layer of pure gold makes the wire tarnish-resistant, and it should be cared for just like the expensive version. Gold-filled wire should be buffed with a soft, clean cloth (such as flannel) and stored in a dry place. Placing tissue paper around your gold-filled wire will minimize exposure to humidity and prevent scratching while it's being stored.

Gold-plated wire exists, but only a microscopic film of karat gold is applied to the outside of the wire, rather than an actual layer.

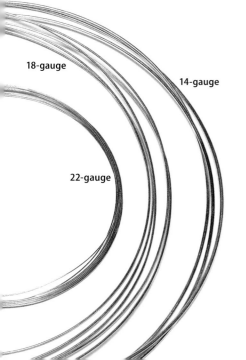

18-gauge

14-gauge

22-gauge

Safety basics

Do:

- Wear eye protection when working with metals and metalsmithing tools.
- Wear a dust mask when working with materials and tools that generate particulates.
- Work in a well-ventilated area.
- Wear protective gloves when handling caustic materials or chemicals.
- Wear a nonflammable apron to protect your clothing.
- Tie back long hair.
- Read all Manufacturer Safety Data Sheets (MSDSs) before using a new material, and keep a copy of the MSDS for any material you use.

Don't:

- Wear open-toed shoes. Dropped tools or hot metal can cause injury.
- Wear loose sleeves, scarves, or other clothing that might get caught in machinery or catch fire.
- Wear long chains or bracelets that might get caught in machinery.
- Use tools or chemicals in ways that are contrary to the manufacturer's intended purpose.

Basics

Temper

The temper of wire is it's hardness, or malleability. Silver and gold wires can be purchased at different levels of hardness, such as dead-soft, half-hard, or full-hard. When working with metal, you want it to be pliable enough to manipulate, yet strong enough to hold its shape. Working with wire strengthens it; this is called work-hardening. Additional strength comes with hammering after you've formed your shape. The trick is to use wire that is soft enough to work with but becomes hard enough to hold the final shape. You likely will want to work with half-hard wire the majority of the time. When connecting elements with double-wrapped loops, the act of wrapping the loops is enough manipulation to fully work-harden the wire so it is at its maximum strength. If you used full-hard wire, it could be too difficult to manipulate. If you use dead-soft wire, it could only become half-hard after wrapping, so it would not maintain its shape as well. Most projects in this book will specify which temper works best for each project.

Wire gauge conversion chart

Gauge size	Diameter (inches)	Diameter (mm)
10	0.102	2.6
12	0.081	2.1
14	0.064	1.6
16	0.051	1.3
18	0.040	1.0
20	0.032	0.8
22	0.025	0.6
24	0.020	0.5
26	0.016	0.4
28	0.013	0.32
30	0.010	0.26

Gauge

Wire gauge is the measure of a wire's thickness, or diameter. The higher the gauge number, the thinner the wire. Thicker wire is more difficult to work with, while thinner wire has less strength.

Thick wire, such as 12- and 14-gauge wire, is most appropriate for projects where strength is a necessary element of the design, such as bangle bracelets. For projects and components that need to be strong, but not quite as sturdy or bulky – such as clasps – 16- and 18-gauge wire is more appropriate. 20- and 22-gauge wire is commonly used for most jewelry-making elements, and is perfect for loops and findings. Finer wires are used with small-holed beads, or for decorative elements.

An American-standard wire gauge displays gauges on one side and the corresponding-diameter decimal measurements on the other. A gauge is measured by the width of each slot on the perimeter of the tool, not by the size of the hole.

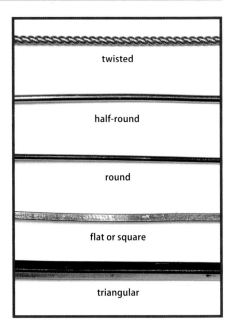

Shape

Wire also comes in a variety of shapes, ranging from the traditional round profile to half-round, flat or square, triangular, and twisted. You can make your own twisted wire by twisting two pieces together.

TOOLS

If you love tools, there's no limit to what you can buy. The jewelry-making world keeps finding more and better ways to create beautiful pieces. The essentials that you absolutely have to have are pliers and cutters. We've included some of the more fundamental tools here, but when it comes to advanced tools, such as torches or rolling mills, it's best to do research and find the equipment that matches your budget and needs.

Pliers

Pliers are necessary for most wire working tasks, including gripping and bending wire, and creating loops. There are also many specialty pliers, such as stone-setters, ring openers, and combinations that might be perfect for your needs. When purchasing pliers, inspect the jaws to see that they are smooth and even, look for a solid joint with a little give or wiggle, and try out the handle. When you spend a lot of time with tools in your hand, comfort becomes increasingly important. Here are some of the basic types of pliers and what they do.

Chainnose pliers have flat inner jaws, great for gripping wire to shape it, or working in conjunction with another type of pliers, to make loops or to open and close jump rings.

Flatnose pliers are similar to chainnose pliers and can be used in the same manner, but have flat outer jaws, making it easier to make sharper bends in the wire.

Bentnose, or bent chainnose pliers, are also close to chainnose pliers, but have a slight bend near the tips. Many jewelry makers prefer these pliers because they find them easier to use than the straight chainnose variety.

Nylon-jaw pliers are another relative of chainnose pliers. These pliers feature replaceable nylon lining on the jaws, which protects wire from marks left by tools and is useful for straightening wire. You can achieve similar results by covering your pliers with tape or Tool Magic, but eventually wear and tear will affect the protection those aids offer. These are particularly useful with wires that have a thin coating of color that could easily scratch off, such as niobium.

Roundnose pliers are critical for making loops and bends. These pliers have conical jaws, perfect for shaping wire.

Saws

Jeweler's saws have two components, an adjustable U-shaped frame with a handle, and a blade. You can use a variety of different blade sizes or thicknesses in the saw; use stronger blades for thicker metal. Saws are great for cutting shapes from metal and sawing through coils to make jump rings.

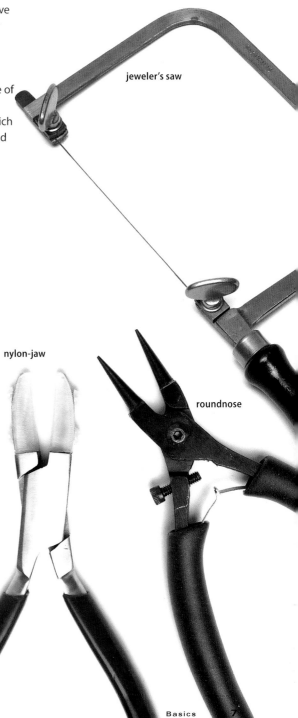

jeweler's saw

bent chainnose

chainnose

nylon-jaw

flatnose

roundnose

Basics

bevel

semi-flush

flush

Cutters

Depending on the type of work you do, you'll need different cutters for your jewelry making. If you file all your ends, a stronger cutter with a less refined finish is appropriate. If you use a lot of jump rings, a saw is essential.

Side cutters are the most common type of cutters. As the name implies, these cutters have blades that are parallel to their handles. Some side cutters have blades that are tilted slightly upward. These are useful because they can cut wire from many angles. Side cutters produce a wide variety of cuts, each with their own strengths and weaknesses. All the cutters included here are usually found as side cutters. End cutters, which have blades set perpendicular to the handles, are usually used to cut heavier elements and aren't commonly used for wirework.

Bevel cutters are economical, can cut very thick gauges of wire, and last longer than many other types of cutters. However, bevel cutters leave both ends of your wire pinched at a slant. (Hence the word "bevel," which means "an incline or slant.") Also, you must squeeze bevel cutters harder than some other types of side cutters. If you want the ends of your wires to be flat, you will have to file them substantially.

Semi-flush cutters leave less of a slant or bur on wire ends than bevel cutters. One side of the cut will be almost flush,

while the other side will be beveled. These cutters are good for beginners to use on a daily basis.

Flush cutters leave even less of a bevel, and **super-flush** (aka ultra-flush) cutters are even better than flush cutters. They produce a flatter cut and require even less energy to use. However, in exchange for their tremendous cutting ability, super-flush cutters lose strength, so you can use them only for wire finer than 18-gauge.

Double-flush cutters leave virtually no bur on either side of the wire, saving you time if you want your wire ends to be perfectly flat. Double-flush cutters work well for making jump rings from wire coils. As you might expect, double-flush cutters work only on thinner gauges of wire, 18-gauge and finer.

Jewelry-making scissors are used to cut sheet solder into pallions (see p. 12). Since solder is very hard, never use wire cutters to cut sheet solder; you'll quickly dull them.

Hammers and mallets

While one hammer might be sufficient for beginners, there's a wide variety of jewelry-making hammers out there, and some will make certain tasks much easier.

Ball-peen and **cross-peen hammers** are the most common jewelry-making hammers. Ball-peen hammers have flat

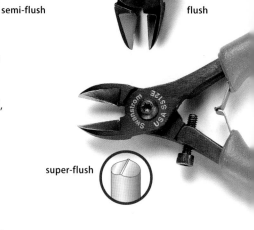

super-flush

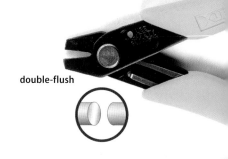

double-flush

scissors

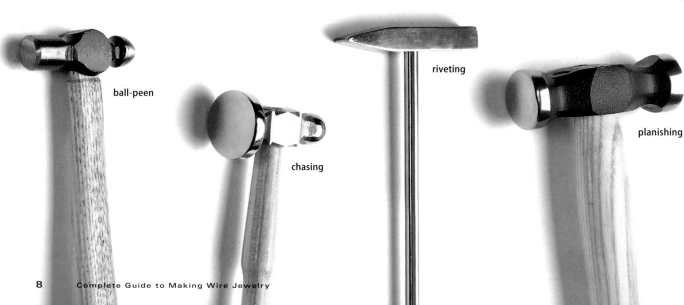

ball-peen

chasing

riveting

planishing

8   *Complete Guide to Making Wire Jewelry*

heads on one end, and domed round heads on the other. Cross-peen hammers have a rectangular head instead of the round head. These hammers are great for shaping and texturing metal.

A **chasing hammer** is struck against tools, like stamps and punches, to make indentations and marks on the metal. It is a modified version of the ball-peen hammer.

A **riveting hammer** can also be used with tools, or to add texture to a piece of metal, but its real purpose is to shape and flatten the rivets used in cold connections. The angled head pushes the metal out with each blow, flaring the rivet heads perfectly.

A **planishing hammer** smooths and flattens the surface of metal. Although other hammers can be used for this purpose, planishing hammers have two flat, round, smooth heads. Keep your planishing heads smooth by never using them with your steel tools. The hard steel will mar the shiny surfaces.

Nylon and **rawhide mallets** are used to pound and form metal without marking it. The head materials cushion the metal while it's being struck. Some rawhide mallets need to be conditioned before they are used, so they don't leave marks.

Bench blocks and anvils

A bench block, or steel block, provides a hard, smooth surface on which to hammer or planish your pieces. An anvil is similarly hard, but has different surfaces, such as a tapered horn, to help forge wire into different shapes.

dapping block and punches

Dapping block

A dapping block, or doming block, is a steel block with a series of concave circles set into its surface. You can use a mallet in conjunction with dapping punches to pound metal pieces into the indentations, giving them a rounded form.

Dowels and mandrels

Dowels are circular rods, frequently made of wood, that jewelry makers use for shaping wire into coils and rings. Mandrels are made of steel, plastic, or wood, and have a smooth or stepped taper, so that rings and coils can be easily measured and removed.

Jewelry makers are frequently creative with their dowels and mandrels and often

use other tools, like punches or knitting needles, as dowels and mandrels.

Drills and punches

Drills and punches are used together to make holes in metal surfaces. First, a center punch (a steel rod with a pointed end) is used to make a dimple in the metal where the hole will be drilled. This dimple keeps the drill bit in place, so it doesn't travel over the surface of the metal and mar it. Then the drill is used to create the hole itself.

Tube wringer

A tube wringer is a crank-operated tool used to wring the last little bit of product from tubes of caulk or paint. The ridged edges are great for shaping wire. They are commonly found at hardware stores.

rawhide mallet

Choosing a hammer for planishing wire

There are special considerations when choosing a hammer to planish wire. A planishing hammer could be used, the face being a desirable shape already. The only drawbacks are that planishing hammers are a bit heavy for wire applications and often have less-than-comfortable handles.

Instead, an 8–10 oz. (226.8–283.5g) chasing hammer with a slightly domed face will work well. Its domed face means that it should not scar the wire when it's struck.

If your hammer does have sharp edges, it's possible to round off the edges on a grinder. Follow-up by sanding and polishing to achieve a smooth finish. Any marks left on the hammer face will transfer to your work, so keep the face smooth and mirror-finished.

To planish wire in tight spaces, use the flat face of a small, lightweight riveting hammer. Keep in mind, like larger chasing hammers, the edges may need to be rounded to prevent transferring edge marks to the wire when you strike the surface.

Basics

files

stamp set

Stamp set

A stamp is a metal tool used for making an impression on metal surfaces. The stamp is held above the metal's surface, then struck with a mallet, forcing it into the metal and leaving an impression on the surface. For clean, clear stamping, always place the metal to be stamped on a steel bench block before striking.

Draw plate

A draw plate is a metal or wooden plate with holes drilled through the surface. Wire and wire chains can be pulled through the holes to make them a uniform size and shape. This decreases the diameter of the chain or wire.

tips on stamping

- Place the anvil or bench block on a solid surface at a comfortable height.
- Wear magnifiers.
- Make a directional mark on a stamp to indicate its orientation.
- Create a guideline with a marker or pencil to line up stamps.
- Adjust the design stamp until the entire design is in contact with the metal to be stamped.
- Hold the stamp firm and steady so it doesn't skid when struck, creating a blurry or ghosted image.
- Use a dropping motion with the mallet.

Torches

Torches are necessary for annealing and soldering wire components. They differ greatly in price range, temperature, and fuel. A wealth of material on torches is available, and those interested in using one should seek advice from trusted, knowledgeable sources.

Flex shafts and Dremels

These handy little motorized tools operate much like a drill with different attachments. Using different heads, you can drill, sand, or buff your piece. Most of the tasks these tools perform can be accomplished with hand tools and elbow grease, but many jewelers appreciate them for the time they can save.

Files

Metal files are used to refine and shape the edges of metal and wire surfaces. In most cases, they are essential for professional-looking jewelry.

TECHNIQUES

Making plain loops

Trim the wire or head pin ⅜ in. (9.5mm) above the top bead. Make a right-angle bend close to the bead [1]. Grab the wire's tip with roundnose pliers. The tip of the wire should be flush with the pliers. Roll the wire to form a half circle. Release the wire [2]. Reposition the pliers in the loop and continue rolling [3]. The finished loop should form a centered circle above the bead [4].

Making a wrapped loop

Trim the wire 1¼ in. (32mm) above the object. Use the tip of your chainnose pliers to grasp the wire directly above the object. Bend the wire into a right angle [5]. Switch to roundnose pliers and grasp the horizontal portion of the wire near the bend, and then bend the wire over the top jaw of the pliers [6]. Reposition the pliers so that the lower jaw fits inside of this half loop. Curve the wire around the bottom jaw of the pliers to make a complete loop [7]. Keep the lower jaw of the roundnose pliers in the loop and wrap the tail around the wire stem above the object [8]. Trim the excess wire, and use chainnose pliers to press the cut end close to the wrap.

Opening and closing jump rings

Hold the jump ring with two pairs of chainnose pliers [9]. To open the jump ring, bring one pair of pliers toward you and push the other pair away from you [10]. Reverse the steps to close the jump ring.

Sawing

To thread a saw blade, insert the blade with the teeth of the blade facing down and away from the handle, into the top wing nut of the saw frame, and tighten the wing nut [11]. Place the handle in the hollow of your shoulder, and apply pressure to the saw frame against your bench pin [12]. Maintaining pressure, insert the bottom of the saw blade into the wing nut closest to the handle, and tighten the wing nut.

The blade should be taut and should make a high-pitched "ping" when plucked with your thumbnail. If you get a dull sound, reinstall your blade while putting pressure on the saw frame. Lubricate the blade with beeswax.

When sawing, sit in an erect posture with the top of your workbench at upper-chest level [13]. Slouching or having your work too low causes back and wrist strain and leads to increased broken saw blades.

To saw, grip the saw frame loosely in your hand. Use long, smooth motions with as much of the blade as possible. The blade will work best when it's perpendicular to

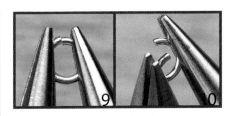

the metal **[14]**. Don't put excessive pressure on the saw frame. Turn corners by slowly sawing in place while turning the metal; trying to turn the saw will break the blade.

Piercing

Use a center punch and mallet on a bench block to create a shallow dimple in the section of the metal you want to remove **[15]**. Place the metal on a piece of wood. Secure the metal with a clamp, lubricate the drill bit with beeswax or Bur Life, and drill a hole using the dimple as a guide **[16]**.

Remove one end of the saw blade from the saw frame. Slide the blade through the hole in the metal, then reinsert the blade into the frame, and tighten **[17]**. Saw out the inside section of the metal. Remove one end of the blade from the saw frame to remove the metal piece. Refine any rough edges with small files.

Making your own jump rings

Select a dowel with a diameter that matches the inside diameter of the jump rings you want to make. Drill a hole through one end of the dowel, or saw a slot in the end of the dowel. Insert the end of the wire into the hole or slot to anchor it in place. Wrap the wire around the dowel, keeping the coils tight together **[18]**.

Cut the wire at the end that anchors the spring. Slide the spring to the opposite end of the dowel.

Secure the dowel against the V notch in your bench pin, and use a jeweler's saw to cut a shallow, vertical slot at the end of the dowel to guide your blade as you cut the spring.

Hold the spring and dowel with your nondominant hand. Saw through the top of the spring, feeding the spring toward the slot in the dowel **[19]**. Be careful not to cut the jump rings in half, and be sure to have a catch tray or stretched apron below your bench pin to catch the falling rings as you cut them apart.

Annealing

Annealing restores malleability to work-hardened metal. Place the metal on a soldering pad, flux it, and heat it with a torch. When the metal has a dull, rose-colored glow and the flux turns clear and glassy, it is annealed. (Immediately remove the heat when you see the color, or you'll burn or melt the metal. Dim or turn off the lights to help you see this color change.) Quench the metal in water, and then soak it in pickle to remove oxides and flux residue.

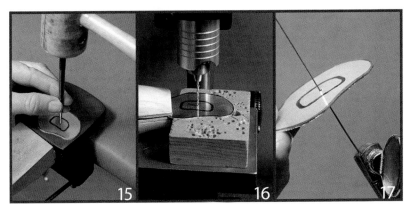

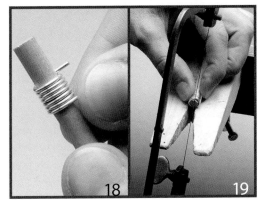

Basics

Soldering
Tools and materials

Solder is a metal alloy that is used to join two pieces of metal. You can buy solder as wire, paste, or sheet. All the projects in this book use sheet solder, which is cut into little pieces called pallions [20, 21]. Solder is available in different grades, ranging from extra hard to extra easy. The harder the solder, the slower it melts. For that reason, if there is more than one solder join in a piece, solder the first one using hard solder, the second using medium solder, and the third using easy solder.

Flux is available as a liquid powder or paste, and is used to coat a surface before solder is applied. Flux helps prevent oxides from forming on the metal when it is heated, which helps solder flow properly.

A **torch** is used to heat the solder and the pieces you wish to join.

Always use a **fire-resistant surface**, like a fire brick or charcoal block, and work in a well-ventilated area.

Water is used for quenching and rinsing the pieces. Fill two heat-resistant bowls: one to quench the piece after soldering, and the other to rinse off the pickle.

A **solder pick** is an awl-like tool with a metal tip and an insulated handle (such as wood) used to move and pick up solder while soldering. Solder doesn't stick to the metals used in solder picks, like steel, titanium, and tungsten carbide.

Pickle cleans the metal and dissolves the flux after the piece is fired. It is slightly acidic, so use it in a well-ventilated area, and take care to keep it off clothes, skin, and other surfaces.

Use **copper tongs** with pickle, as stainless steel will cause a copper plating of other metals in the pickle.

A **warming pot** can be used to keep pickle at a warmer temperature, which makes it work more quickly.

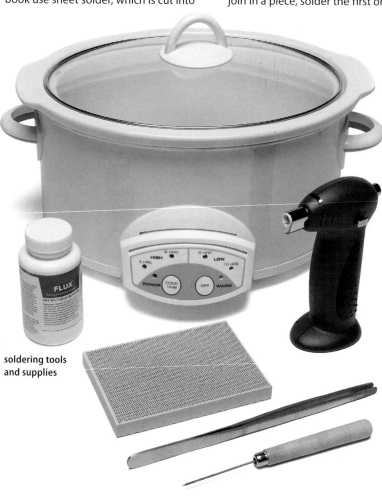

soldering tools and supplies

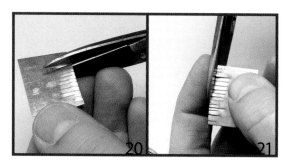

tips on soldering

- Use magnifiers so that you can see your work.
- Always have a soldering pick in hand when heating small elements, since they melt quickly.
- Always heat the flux until it is melted BEFORE you place the solder.
- Use a small- or medium-tipped torch, and heat the flux and elements to be soldered slowly and gently—this will keep the flux from rapidly bubbling and moving your elements and solder out of place.
- Keep your solder grades separate or organized to minimize confusion and prevent meltdowns.
- Remember, practice is the key.

Prepare the join

All metal surfaces must be clean in order for solder to flow. Clean metal by sanding it with 400-grit sandpaper and rinsing it. The surfaces must be in complete contact with each other in order for the solder to join them – solder will not fill holes or gaps.

Flux and heat

Flux the area to be soldered to prevent oxidation. You can apply flux with a dropper or paint it on with a brush [22]. Place the solder on the join and heat the entire piece, not just the solder. Keep the torch moving in a circular motion [23]. Solder will flow toward the source of the heat, so once the solder begins to flow you can use your torch to direct it where you want it to go. When the solder flows, you'll see a flash of silver and it will move into the join. When this happens, immediately remove the heat.

Pickle and rinse

Once the solder flows, quench the piece in water, and place it in a pickle solution [24] to remove oxidation and flux residue until it is clean and white (for silver). Rinse the piece in clean water.

Finishing
Sanding

To remove scratches from metal, use a series of sandpapers, starting with a coarse grit and progressing to finer grits. A 220-grit sandpaper is good to begin with; progress through 320, 400, 600, and up to 1200 grit or higher, depending on the finish you desire.

Types of finishes
Satin finish

Sand the metal with progressively finer sandpapers up to 600 grit. Use soapy water and a brass brush to lightly rub the metal. Alternatively, lightly rub with a

24

piece of fine steel wool or an abrasive scouring pad.

Tumble polish

Sand the metal with progressively finer-grit sandpapers up to 600 grit. Place 1 lb. (454g) of stainless steel shot into the rotary tumbler's barrel. Pour in water to cover the shot, then add a pinch of burnishing compound. Place your jewelry in the tumbler and seal the barrel. Turn on the tumbler, and let it run for 2–3 hours or overnight. Pour the contents of the tumbler into a sieve over a sink, and rinse with cool water. Remove your jewelry and dry it. Dry the shot before storing it.

High polish

Sand the metal with progressively finer grits up to 1200 grit. Use a flex shaft or a buffing machine with a fabric wheel attachment, or "buff." Jeweler's polishing compounds are applied to the buff. Each compound should be applied only to a dedicated buff. The two most common types of compound are tripoli, which removes fine scratches, and red rouge, which polishes the metal. Scrub the metal in soapy water with a toothbrush to remove polishing-compound residue before moving on to the next compound.

Liver of sulfur patina

Polish your piece before patinating. If you tumble-polish your piece after patinating, reserve the used shot for future patinated pieces; the liver of sulfur residue will contaminate other pieces.

Oil and dirt on the piece can affect the patina; use a degreasing soap to clean the metal before patinating.

Prepare a liver of sulfur solution according to the manufacturer's instructions. Using dedicated tongs, dip the metal in the solution for a few seconds, then rinse the metal in cool water to stop the chemical reaction. For a darker patina, continue to dip and rinse the metal. Use a brass brush with soapy water to remove or modify the patina. By using different temperatures and amounts of water to make the liver of sulfur solution, you can achieve different colors of patina; experiment to find the result you prefer. You can also apply liver of sulfur to selected areas of the metal with a small paintbrush.

Finish like a pro

Looking for an eye-catching showcase finish? Follow these important steps to ensure a finish on par with the pros.

1 Look the piece over for sharp and protruding wire ends. Clip them flush. A good pair of flush cutters will reduce the need for sanding, but when necessary, emery boards are a convenient and economical choice.

2 If you wish to remove some of the surface oxides, brass wool is a valuable choice. It will rub some of the black coloration off to reveal silver again. Brass wool will not rust if left undetected in crevices, unlike steel wool. Brass wool can be found at marine supply stores.

3 Polish the piece with a polishing cloth that has been charged with tripoli. This will remove the subtle scratches from the brass wool that dull the finish, as well as smooth out some of the work marks from pliers and planishing. Some work marks will certainly remain and are indicative of handmade jewelry. Follow up by washing the piece in warm, soapy water.

4 Polish the piece with a cloth charged with red rouge. Jewelry-making suppliers carry cloths that are precharged with tripoli and red rouge, or you can do it the old-fashioned way by purchasing blocks of tripoli or rouge, and applying them with a chamois cloth.

5 Wash the piece in warm, soapy water again to remove the greasy polish residue. Scrub the compound out of any crevices with a soft toothbrush. Dry the piece with a soft cloth.

Coils and Shapes

Wire is a malleable medium, allowing artists to sculpt all kinds of wonderful coils, links, and shapes. Even the most basic wire jewelry requires the maker to create simple forms, such as loops, curves, and spirals. Perfecting those shapes, expanding and repeating them, is what transforms the pieces from ordinary to spectacular. This chapter focuses on basic skills, but the repetitive nature of some projects will advance your level of craftsmanship. In this section of the book, wire is used as a primary design element – the shapes and capabilities of wire are the backbone of the design, whether the wire is used to make a neckwire for an art bead choker, a pair of dangling earrings that dance when you move, or a timeless necklace of graduated, domed spirals.

Wrapped
in gold

*A basic wire-wrapping technique forms a
choker to showcase an art glass bead.*

by Linda Augsburg

A cylindrical glass bead sparked the inspiration for this easy wirework choker.
Choose any large bead – round or oblong, glass, ceramic, or metal – and
add a cluster of complementary smaller beads. The choker shown here
has a 1⅝-inch (41mm) focal bead, two ⅜-inch (9.5mm) sections of crystals, and two
8-inch (20.3cm) coils. Using basic coiling and wrapped-loop techniques with a
handmade clasp allows every component to integrate seamlessly into the whole.

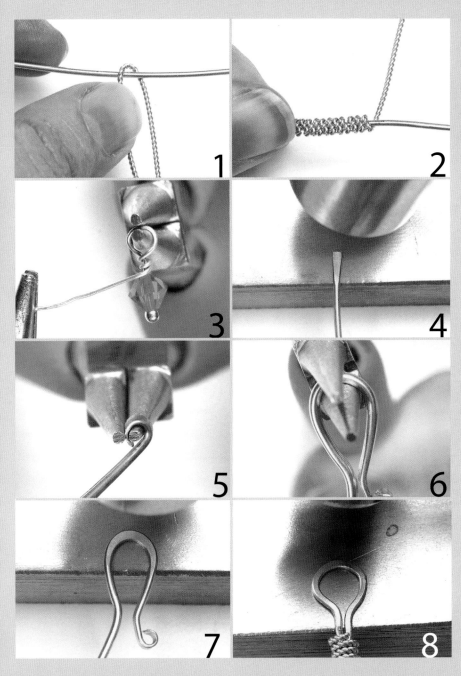

1

2

3

4

5

6

7

8

part of your roundnose pliers to make a hook about ¾ inch (19mm) from the loop **[6]**. Hammer the top of the hook to harden it **[7]**. Form a second small loop in the opposite direction on the wire just beyond the small loop on the opposite side (see detail photo, below) and hammer it slightly to harden it. This loop will keep the coil in place.

Form the eye loop. Slide the coils and beads to the hook end. Applying slight pressure to the coil, mark the 16-gauge wire for cutting 2 inches (5.1cm) beyond the end of the coil. Cut the wire. Form a ⅜-inch (9.5mm)-diameter loop perpendicular to the hook with a ¼-inch (6.5mm) tail at the bottom. Hammer the loop slightly, pressing the coil away from the loop **[8]**. Slide the coil over the tail.

Finish. Try on the necklace; shape it to your neck.

materials

- 4 yards (3.7m) of 22-gauge gold-filled round twisted wire
- 18 inches (45.7cm) of 16-gauge gold-filled half-hard round wire
- 40mm art glass bead
- 36 or more crystal beads in assorted shapes, sizes, and colors to complement art bead
- 36 or more 22- or 24-gauge decorative gold-filled head pins

tools and supplies

- wire cutters
- chainnose pliers
- roundnose pliers
- bench block or anvil
- hammer

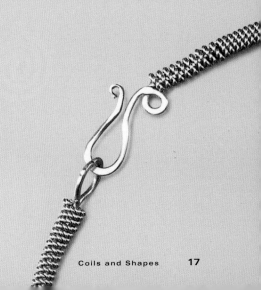

Coil the wire. Cut a 2-yard (1.8m) length of the twisted wire. Bend it in half. Place the 16-gauge wire against the fold in the twisted wire **[1]**. With your dominant hand, use your fingers to wrap the twisted wire in a tight coil around the 16-gauge wire **[2]**. When you reach the end of the first half of the twisted wire, turn the piece around and wrap the other half. When finished, slide the coil off the 16-gauge wire. Repeat with a second 2-yard length of twisted wire.

Make the crystal dangles. Slide each crystal bead on a head pin. Make a wrapped loop large enough to accommodate 16-gauge wire above each crystal **[3]**.

String the necklace. Center the focal bead on the 16-gauge wire, then string an equal number of crystal dangles on each end. Slide a coil of wire on each end. Curve the wire to fit your neck, determine the desired finished length minus the clasp, and trim an equal length from each coil as necessary. Do not cut the 16-gauge wire at this time.

Form the hook. Slide everything to one end of the 16-gauge wire. Hammer the opposite end against a bench block or anvil to form a ³⁄₁₆-inch (5mm) paddle shape **[4]**. With roundnose pliers, turn the end to form a small loop **[5]**. Use the wide

Flowing ringlets

Like a mountain spring, these remarkably easy earrings are refreshingly beautiful.

by Lisa Niven Kelly

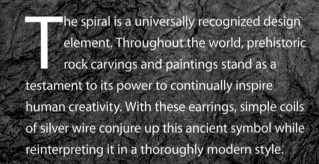

The spiral is a universally recognized design element. Throughout the world, prehistoric rock carvings and paintings stand as a testament to its power to continually inspire human creativity. With these earrings, simple coils of silver wire conjure up this ancient symbol while reinterpreting it in a thoroughly modern style.

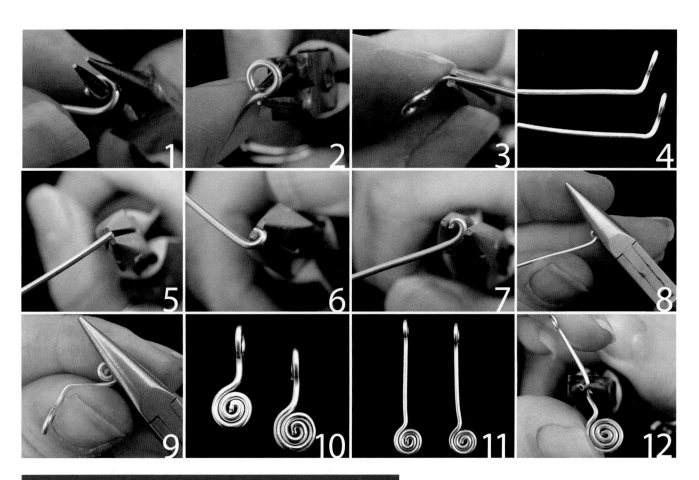

making ear wires

Cut a 3-inch (7.6cm) piece of 20-gauge sterling silver wire.

Make a coil on one end with only two rotations. Grip the wire just below the coil at the midpoint in the jaw of your roundnose pliers. Bend the wire away from the coil until it comes around and touches the coil's back [a], creating the bottom loop. Form the arc in the ear wire by bending the wire around a 3/8-inch (9.5mm)- diameter mandrel or pliers [b]. Hammer the coil, the bottom loop, and the arc on the ear wire to work-harden them, which will ensure that they will keep their shapes [c].

Use a file or concave cutting bur to round the ends of the ear wires. Patinating the ear wires may cause irritation. To avoid this, apply a warm solution of liver of sulfur with a paintbrush to the coils only.

Make a basic top loop. Cut two 1½-inch (38mm) pieces of 18-gauge sterling silver wire. Grip the wire's tip with the base of your roundnose pliers (1/8 inch/3mm jaw diameter). Roll the wire to form a basic loop. Release the wire, and reposition the pliers to finish the loop [1]. Position the pliers where the loop meets the stem. Gently squeeze at this spot while shifting the loop backward to center it on the wire [2]. Measure 1/8 inch (3mm) from the base of the loop, grip the wire with the tip of your chainnose pliers, and bend the wire 90 degrees [3]. This bend will make the stem of the wire perpendicular to the loop. Repeat with the second piece of wire [4].

Make the coils in the short dangles. To coil the wire stem so there is no hole at its center, grip the tip of the stem with the very tip of your chainnose pliers [5]. Rotate the pliers to make a tiny U-shaped bend [6]. Release the pliers, and squeeze the bend closed [7]. Reposition the pliers to grasp the bend horizontally near the pliers' hinge [8]. Rotate your pliers while pushing the stem with your fingers to form a coil [9]. Coil the stem to the 90-degree bend [10].

Make the long dangles. Cut two 2-inch (5.1cm) pieces of 18-gauge sterling silver wire. Follow steps 1 and 2 to make a basic top loop on each wire. Measure 1/2 inch (13mm) from the base of the loop, bend the stem at a 90-degree angle, and coil the stem to that bend [11].

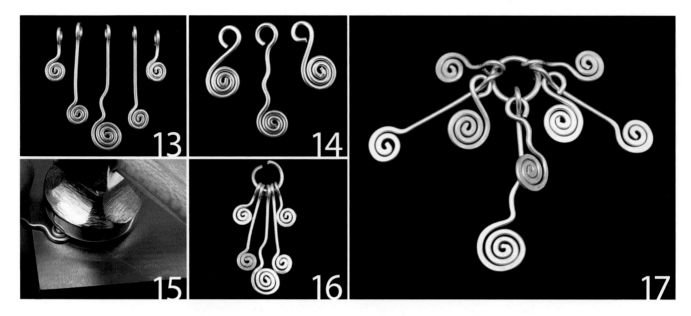

For the center dangle, cut a 3-inch (7.6cm) piece of 18-gauge wire. Make a top loop. Measure 1¾ inch (4.4cm) from the base of the loop, bend the wire at a 90-degree angle, and coil the stem to that bend. Form an S-shaped wave in the stem by gripping the wire in the base of your roundnose pliers (⁵⁄₃₂–³⁄₁₆ inch/4–5mm jaw diameter). Push the coil in one direction while pulling the loop in the opposite direction **[12]**. Here are the first five dangles in graduated order **[13]**.

Make the figure 8 dangles. Cut two 2-inch (5.1cm) pieces of 18-gauge sterling silver wire. Grasp the very end of the wire with your roundnose pliers, and roll it to make a loop (this loop will not be centered on the wire). Coil the stem in the direction opposite the top loop. Repeat with the second wire.

To make a longer figure 8 dangle with a 2-inch (51mm) 18-gauge piece of wire, make a plain top loop as before, but center it. Measure ¼ inch (6.5mm) from the base of the loop, bend the

wire at a 90-degree angle, and coil the stem to that bend. Form an S-shaped wave in the stem with your roundnose pliers as before **[14]**.

Hammer the coils. Use a chasing or planishing hammer to flatten the coils on all the dangles **[15]**. Do not hammer the top loops.

Link the dangles. Use a 10mm outside diameter, 16-gauge sterling silver jump ring to hold the first five dangles in graduated order **[16]**, with the top-loop openings facing the back. Close the jump ring. Open the loop of a small figure 8 dangle. Link it to the loop of a long dangle, and close the figure 8 dangle's loop. Repeat on the other side. Link the longer figure 8 dangle to the center dangle's loop **[17]**. Link the 10mm jump ring to the loop of an ear wire, and close it. Make the second earring as the mirror image of the first.

materials
- sterling silver wire:
  - 3 feet (91.4cm) round, 18 gauge, dead-soft
  - 6 inches (15.2cm) round, 20 gauge, dead-soft
- 2 16 gauge, 10mm outside diameter, sterling silver jump rings

tools and supplies
- flush cutters
- chainnose pliers
- roundnose pliers
- chasing or planishing hammer
- bench block
- bezel mandrel, 10mm-diameter dowel, or stepped-roundnose pliers
- files or concave cutting bur
- liver of sulfur (optional)
- paintbrush (optional)

Turning a new leaf

Use wire-wrapped leaf links to bring variety to your jewelry designs.

by Karen Rakoski

Instead of making round links in your next piece, why not try a leaf shape? A single wire-wrapped leaf link can add an accent, provide color, lighten the weight of a piece, or provide balance to a design. This wire-wrapping technique will get you started on making two basic leaf shapes. One leaf has a center vein, which gives it additional strength so it can support heavier materials. The other leaf is without a center vein and should not be overstressed, or it might pull out of shape. Both leave room for many creative possibilities.

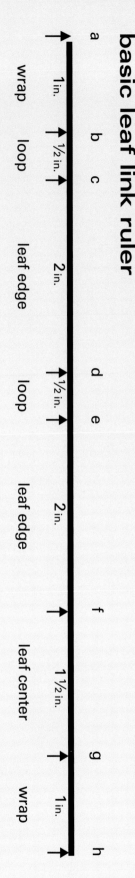

basic leaf link ruler

wrap — 1 in. — a

loop — 1/2 in. — b
— c

leaf edge — 2 in. —

loop — 1/2 in. — d
— e

leaf edge — 2 in. —

— f

leaf center — 1 1/2 in. — g

wrap — 1 in. — h

▲ **Line up a wire with these rulers to mark the points for wrapping your leaf link. Enlarge or reduce the rulers with a photocopier to vary the size of the leaf link.**

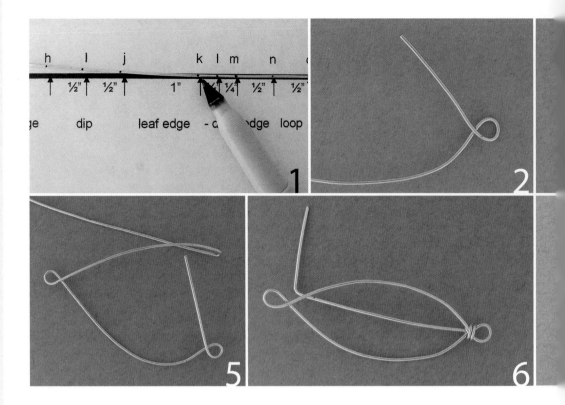

The basic leaf link

Cut and mark the wire. Cut an 8½-inch (21.6cm) piece of 20-gauge wire. If desired, cut extra wire to accommodate variances in wire wrapping. Extra wire can be trimmed in the final step. Lay the wire along the basic leaf link ruler, *left*, and use a permanent marker to mark the points indicated by the arrows **[1]**. First test your marker on a scrap piece of wire to ensure that the marks can be removed from the finished link. The ink of many permanent markers will come off with rubbing alcohol.

Make the first loop. Measure 1 inch (2.5cm) from the wire end, which is indicated on the leaf ruler by the letter **a**. Use roundnose pliers to bend the ½-inch (13mm) section of wire between **marks b** and **c** to make a teardrop-shaped loop so that **marks b** and **c** align. The short end of the wire should cross over the long wire **[2]**.

Curve the leaf edge. Use your thumb to curve the 2-inch (51mm) section between **marks c** and **d [3]**.

Make the top loop. Use roundnose pliers to bend the ½-inch (13mm) section between **marks d** and **e** to make a teardrop loop so **marks d** and **e** align, crossing the longer end of the wire over the curved wire. This is the first leaf edge **[4]**.

Curve the second leaf edge. Use your thumb to curve the 2-inch (51mm) section between **marks e** and **f** outward.

Close the leaf link. Use roundnose pliers to make a tight U bend in the wire at **mark f [5]**. Thread the U bend onto the wire tail left over from the first loop. Move the U bend to the intersection of the first loop. Use flatnose pliers to compress and hold the U bend while wrapping the wire tail (**a–b**) two or three times around the intersection.

Make the center vein. Use roundnose pliers to make a 90-degree bend in the wire at **mark g [6]**. Use flatnose pliers to hold the top loop while wrapping the remaining 1 inch (25.5mm) of wire between **marks g** and **h** two or three times around the intersection **[7]**. Shape the link as desired. Clean off any marks. To curve this link or to make a link with serrated edges, see "Shaping the Leaf Links," or "Serrated Leaf Link," *opposite*.

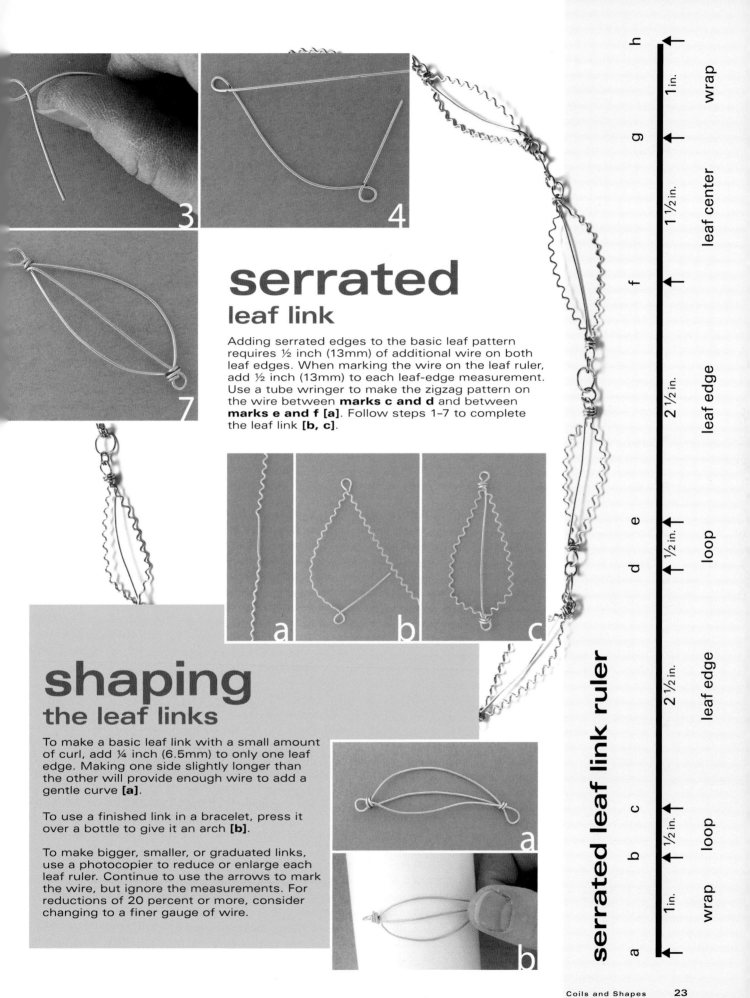

serrated
leaf link

Adding serrated edges to the basic leaf pattern requires ½ inch (13mm) of additional wire on both leaf edges. When marking the wire on the leaf ruler, add ½ inch (13mm) to each leaf-edge measurement. Use a tube wringer to make the zigzag pattern on the wire between **marks c and d** and between **marks e and f [a]**. Follow steps 1–7 to complete the leaf link **[b, c]**.

shaping
the leaf links

To make a basic leaf link with a small amount of curl, add ¼ inch (6.5mm) to only one leaf edge. Making one side slightly longer than the other will provide enough wire to add a gentle curve **[a]**.

To use a finished link in a bracelet, press it over a bottle to give it an arch **[b]**.

To make bigger, smaller, or graduated links, use a photocopier to reduce or enlarge each leaf ruler. Continue to use the arrows to mark the wire, but ignore the measurements. For reductions of 20 percent or more, consider changing to a finer gauge of wire.

serrated leaf link ruler

a		b	c	d	e	f	g	h
1 in.			½ in.		½ in.	1½ in.		1 in.
wrap		loop		2½ in.	loop	leaf center		wrap
				leaf edge		leaf edge		

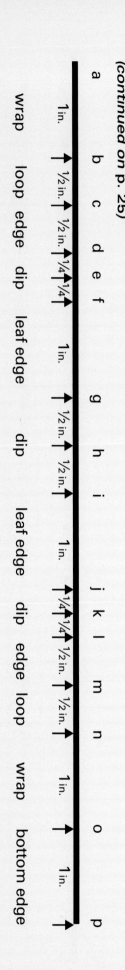

(continued on p. 25)

ginkgo leaf link ruler

mark	measurement	label
a		wrap
b	1 in.	loop
c	½ in.	edge
d	½ in.	dip
e	¼ in.	leaf
f	¼ in.	edge
g	1 in.	dip
h	½ in.	leaf
i	½ in.	edge
j	1 in.	dip
k	¼ in.	edge
l	¼ in.	loop
m	½ in.	edge
n	½ in.	wrap
o	1 in.	bottom edge
p	1 in.	

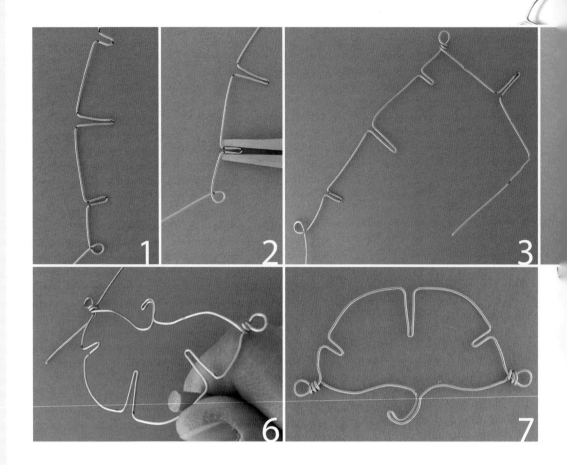

The ginkgo leaf link

Cut and mark the wire. Cut 12 inches (30.5cm) of 20-gauge wire, and lay it along the ginkgo leaf link ruler, *left and right*. Use a permanent marker to mark the wire at the points indicated by the arrows. Test your marker on a scrap piece of wire to ensure that the marks can be removed from the finished link. The ink of many permanent markers will come off with rubbing alcohol.

Make the first loop. Measure 1 inch (2.5cm) from the wire end, which is indicated on the leaf ruler by the letter **a**. Use roundnose pliers to bend the ½-inch (13mm) section of wire between **marks b** and **c**. Make a teardrop-shaped loop so that **marks b** and **c** align. The short wire should cross over the long wire.

Make three U bends. Use roundnose pliers to make a 90-degree bend in the wire at **mark d**. At **mark e**, bend the wire 180 degrees, and at **mark f** make a 90-degree bend. Repeat these three bends at **marks g, h,** and **i** and again at **marks j, k,** and **l**, creating three U bends in the top of the ginkgo leaf link **[1]**. Use flatnose pliers to tighten the U bends **[2]**.

Make the second loop. Use roundnose pliers to make a teardrop-shaped loop between **marks m** and **n** so that **marks m** and **n** align. Cross the long end of the wire over the wire in which you have made the U bends. Use flatnose pliers to hold the loop, and wrap the 1-inch (25.5mm) section of wire between **marks n** and **o** three times around the intersection **[3]**. Gently arch the top of the leaf.

Make the stem. Use roundnose pliers to make a 90-degree bend in the wire at **mark p**. At **mark q**, bend the wire 180 degrees, and at **mark r,** make a 90-degree bend. Use flatnose pliers to tighten the U bend. Use roundnose and chainnose pliers to curl the stem toward the bottom of the leaf **[4]**.

Close the leaf link. Use flatnose pliers to hold the first loop, and wrap the wire end three times around the intersection of the wires **[5]**. Trim any excess wire.

Shape the leaf. Using your thumb and a dowel, round the top and bottom leaf sections **[6]**. Shape the link as desired, and clean off any permanent ink marks **[7]**.

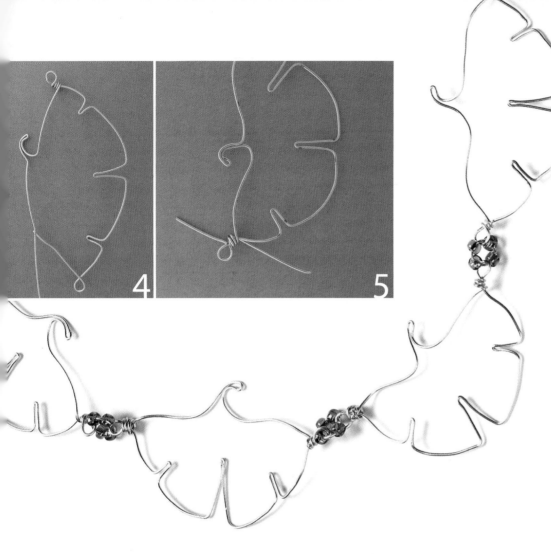

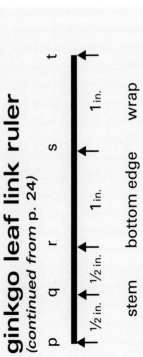

ginkgo leaf link ruler
(continued from p. 24)

t

1 in.

s

1 in.

r

½ in.

q

½ in.

p

wrap

bottom edge

stem

materials

- gold-filled, sterling silver, or craft wire (coated or plain), 20-gauge, round, half-hard:
  - basic link: 8½ inches (21.6cm)
  - serrated link: 9½ inches (24.1cm)
  - ginkgo link: 12 inches (30.5cm)
- split rings or jump rings (optional)

tools and supplies

- wire cutters
- permanent marker
- rubbing alcohol
- chainnose pliers
- flatnose pliers
- roundnose pliers
- tube wringer (optional)
- wooden dowel

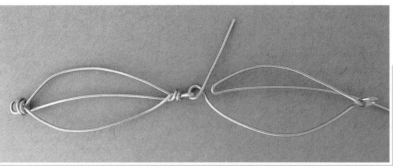

continuous
links

The basic leaf link pattern produces a link with two closed loops. Use split rings, simple double-wrapped loops, or jump rings to join them.

To connect leaf links without using jump rings, rotate the top and bottom loops of two leaf links until the loops are perpendicular to the rest of the link. Make a third basic leaf link as before, up to the U-bend. Then, thread the perpendicular loops of the finished leaves onto each of the teardrop-shaped loops. Complete steps 5–7. Repeat as needed to reach your desired chain length.

Fleur-de-link

Fashion perfectly bound wire links in this flower-inspired chain.

by Lisa Niven Kelly

T ired of wearing the same chain or slide with every pendant in your collection? This wire-wrapped chain gives you the perfect excuse to step beyond the ordinary. Fit for any occasion, it can be dressed up or down depending on the focal element you choose. The pendant is connected to a central jump ring, so you can easily interchange it with other centerpieces.

Curvaceous wire tendrils give this design a lively, playful feel, and the entire chain is created using only 18-gauge wire. The finished chain was soaked in liver of sulfur for a dark patina to give the strand a vintage character. The 18-inch (45.7cm) necklace shown is made up of four major elements: six two-link units, one clasp, a centerpiece unit, and the pendant (stone). These segments are all joined with handmade triple split rings and jump rings.

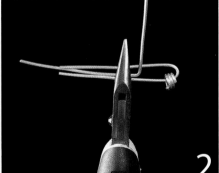
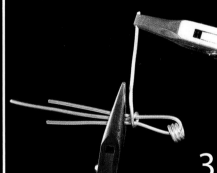

Make the connectors

Make eight triple split rings. Make a 6mm-diameter triple split ring by coiling a 2½-inch (6.4cm) piece of 18-gauge wire around a 6mm dowel three times. Begin and end on the same side of the form and trim any excess wire. Repeat this step to make a total of eight triple split rings. Set them aside.

Editor's Note: If you use roundnose pliers during this step, take into account the tapering of the jaws. In order to get a coil that doesn't taper, you'll need to draw a line around one jaw of the pliers and consistently slide your wire to that spot before wrapping each coil **[1]**.

Make nine jump rings. Form nine 7mm-inside-diameter jump rings using 18-gauge wire.

Create the two-link units

Cut and shape the wires. Cut two 3½-inch (8.9cm) pieces of 18-gauge wire. Bend one of the pieces in half around the thick part of a roundnose pliers to form a U shape. Bend the other wire in half into a sharp right angle using the edge of a chain-nose pliers. Slide one triple split ring onto the U-shaped wire.

Bind the wires together. Hold the right-angle wire against the U-shaped wire so that the right angle is

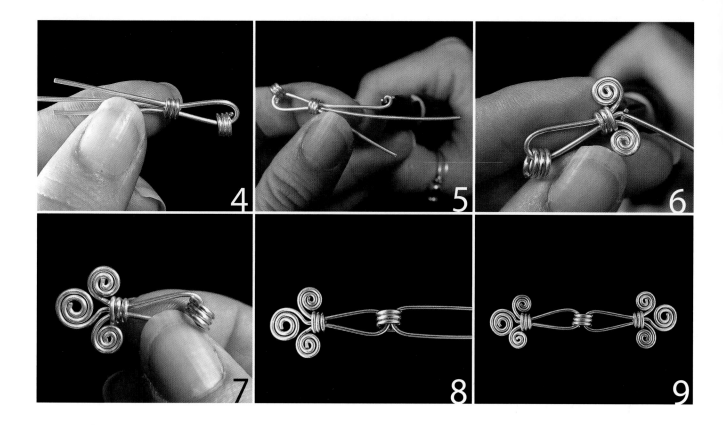

about ½ inch (13mm) away from the base of the U and resembles a backward L. Grasp both wires with chainnose pliers, positioning the pliers a few millimeters to the left of the right-angle bend [2]. Wrap the free end of the right-angle wire (the wrapping wire) around the other wires three times, ending on the same side where you began [3, 4].

Shape decorative coils. There should now be three wire ends sticking out from the binding wrap. With each of the outside wires, use roundnose and chainnose pliers to form two outward-rolling coils [5]. Kink the center wire slightly to one side using chainnose pliers [6]. Form the center wire into a large coil with an interior loop large enough to accommodate a jump ring [7].

Form the second link of the unit. Cut two more 3½-inch (8.9cm) pieces of wire; form a U shape with one of the wires and a right angle with the other as done before. Loop the U-shaped wire through the triple split ring on the first completed link [8]. Now finish making the link by adding a binding wrap and forming the decorative coils, as before [9].

Repeat. Make a total of six of these two-link units.

Form the clasp

Make the clasp pieces. Use a 5-inch (12.7cm) piece of wire to create a U shape. Do not slide a triple split ring onto the U-shaped wire. Use a 3½-inch (8.9cm) piece of wire and position a binding wrap ¾ inch (19mm) away from the base of the U shape (rather than ½ inch/13mm away). This creates a longer U-shaped loop. Bend the U-shaped loop around a cylindrical form to create a hook.

For the adjoining piece of the clasp, make the first link of a two-link unit without adding a triple split ring. The hook end of one clasp piece will slide into the loop end of the other piece [10]. Do not attach them yet.

Create the centerpiece unit

Form the centerpiece unit. This looks similar to the two-link units you made earlier; however, the second link is not looped through the triple split ring of the first – the two links are formed independently. While forming each link, slide a triple split ring onto the U-shaped wire before completing the binding wraps and decorative coils. When the links are complete, connect their triple split rings with one jump ring, which will carry the center drop [11].

Assemble and apply finishing touches

Assemble the necklace. Position three of your two-link units in a horizontal line with the coiled ends touching. Connect the three units by linking their large coils together with jump rings [12]. Repeat with the remaining three two-link units to make a second strand.

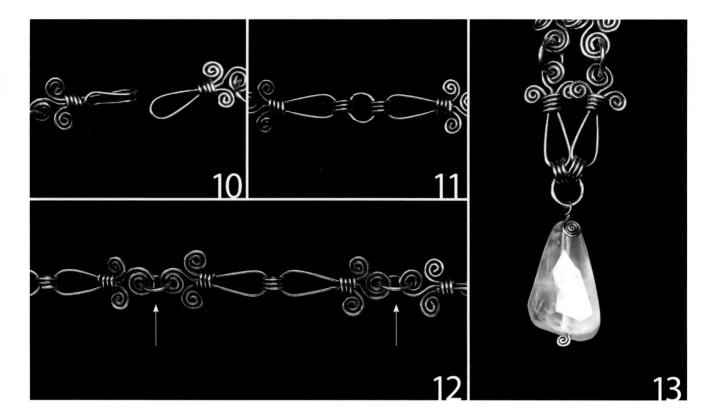

Position the centerpiece unit between the two strands and connect it to them using jump rings. Connect one clasp piece to each end using jump rings.

Solder the jump rings closed (optional). Solder all jump rings closed if desired.

Patinate the necklace (optional). Use liver of sulfur to give the necklace an antiqued look. If you choose to do this, patinate the piece of 22-gauge wire from the next step as well.

Attach the center drop. Cut a 2- to 3-inch (5.1–7.6cm) piece of 22-gauge wire. Form a small coil on one end of the wire. Slide a stone or bead of your choice onto the wire until it rests against the coil. Make a wrapped loop (Basics) above the pendant, attaching the pendant to the center jump ring before you complete the wraps. Cut the remaining wire tail for a clean look, or coil the tail and drape it over the front of the stone for added embellishment **[13]**.

For a more easily interchangeable pendant, attach a second jump ring or wire hook to the center jump ring. Attach your pendant to the second jump ring and carefully open and close the ring to interchange pendants.

materials
- sterling silver wire:
  - 4 yards (3.7m) 18-gauge, round, half-hard
  - 2–3 inches (5.1–7.6cm) 22-gauge, round, half-hard
- pendant bead

tools and supplies
- dowels, 6mm and 7mm
- wire cutters
- chainnose pliers
- roundnose pliers
- jeweler's saw and wooden bench pin or workbench or flush cutters
- files or sanding tool
- soldering materials (optional)
- liver of sulfur (optional)

Wire illusions

Shape a gradation of spirals for this hypnotically alluring necklace.

by Kristi Zevenbergen

uggestive of ethnic jewelry crafted in ancient times, this wire-sculpted necklace is a practice in manipulating large-gauge wire into loops and spirals and carefully planishing areas for handwrought appeal. Domed spiral components draw you into their hypnotic wraps, and curvaceous quad-loops run across the tops of the spirals as linking elements that bring the necklace together.

Quad-loop-link components

Make an S shape. Cut one 3¼-inch (83mm) piece of wire. Using the thickest part of the jaws on your roundnose pliers, grasp the wire at its center. Bend each end of the wire in opposite directions around the base of each jaw of the pliers to form an S shape [1].

Form the first loop. Insert the top jaw of the roundnose pliers into the bottom curve of the S shape. With the pliers pointing toward you, over-complete the bottom loop with the tail pointing to 7 o'clock [2]. (Over-complete the loop by rocking the pliers a quarter turn.)

Form the second loop. Keeping the same side of the work facing you, insert the bottom jaw of the roundnose pliers into the top curve. Over-complete the second loop so the two tails are pointing in opposite directions [3].

Identify the front and back of the work. The back of the work resembles two jump rings sitting next to each other. The front of the work displays an unbroken figure-8 shape.

True-up and planish the first two loops. Reinsert the roundnose pliers into both loops at the same time with the back of the work facing you. True-up the shape, pushing the work down to the base of the pliers and bringing the loops to the same plane

back

back

materials

- 5 yards (4.6m) round, 18-gauge, dead-soft sterling silver wire
- clasp

tools and supplies

- wire cutters
- chainnose pliers
- small roundnose pliers
- bench block
- hammers: chasing, planishing, or riveting (small)
- mandrel, 3.7mm, or knitting needles, size #4 (or equivalent)
- jeweler's saw, 2/0 blades
- liver of sulfur (optional)
- emery boards (optional)
- steel or brass wool (optional)
- precharged polishing cloths, or tripoli and red rouge with chamois cloth (optional)

with no overlapping. Make sure the loops are the same shape and size. Remove the work from your pliers. On the corner of a bench block, carefully planish the front side of the work, avoiding the intersection of the wires and planishing the loops' edges **[4]**.

Form the third loop. With the back of the work facing you, insert the top jaw of the pliers into the top loop and position the bottom jaw of the pliers in the "waist" and to the left of the figure-8 shape. Wrap the wire tail of the top loop counterclockwise around the base of the lower jaw of the pliers. Over-complete this loop with the tail pointing to 11 o'clock **[5]**, repositioning the pliers as necessary.

Form the fourth loop. Turn the work so the long tail points to 12 o'clock, and make the fourth loop as you made the third. Flip the work over to the front **[6]**.

Clip the wire ends and planish. Clip the wire ends at the back, and gently planish the third and fourth loops, again avoiding the central intersection **[7]**.

Repeat. Make a total of ten quad-loop-link components.

Graduated spiral components

Cut wire. Cut one 9-inch (22.9cm) piece of wire for the center spiral component. Cut two pieces of each of the following lengths: 8 inches (20.3cm), 7 inches (17.8cm), 6½ inches (16.5cm), and 5½ inches (14.0cm). Cut four 6-inch (15.2cm) pieces. Using a permanent marker, mark each wire at a point 2 inches (5.1cm) from one end.

Make the first three loops of the link. To make the initial S shape, as in the four-loop components, grasp the 9-inch (22.9cm) piece of wire at the mark you have made, rather than at the center. This will leave a longer tail to form the spiral in the next step. Make the second loop exactly as in part 1. Make the third loop as in part 1, but use the short tail. Clip the wire end of the third loop, and gently planish only that loop **[8]**.

Form the spiral. Work on the piece with the back facing you. Grasp the end of the long tail

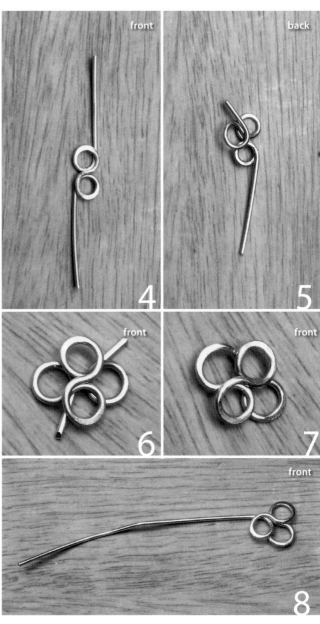

with chainnose pliers, and turn the wire very tightly around the tip of the pliers to form a tight core for the spiral. Grasp the core horizontally with your pliers, and feed the wire onto the core by turning the core, rather than by stretching the wire. As you turn the core, form the wire around it with your fingers. Wrap each spiral slightly on top of the previous one to achieve a convex appearance from the front. This is subtle and will take practice. Flip the work over to the front [9].

Repeat. Make a total of 13 spiral components using the other lengths of wire cut previously.

Jump rings

Make 72 jump rings. Form 72 jump rings by wrapping an 18-gauge wire around a 3.7mm dowel. A 1 foot (30.5cm) length of 18-gauge wire will yield approximately 21 jump rings on this size mandrel. Use approximately 4 feet (1.2m) of wire to make all the jump rings. Additional jump rings can be made to add length to the necklace.

Assembling and finishing the necklace

Assemble the necklace. Place the largest spiral component in the center of your work surface. Lay out the remaining 12 spiral components, six to each side of the center, graduating from largest in the front of the necklace to smallest in the back. Connect all components with two jump rings between each [10].

Lay out the quad-loop links, five on each side of the connected spiral components. Join all the links with two jump rings between each [11]. Attach the remaining jump rings in sets of two to each side. If more length is desired, use additional pairs of jump rings two at a time on each side until the piece reaches the desired length. Attach a clasp of your choice with a pair of jump rings [12].

Patinate (optional). Give the necklace an antiqued look by soaking it in a warm solution of liver of sulfur and water. This will give the piece more depth.

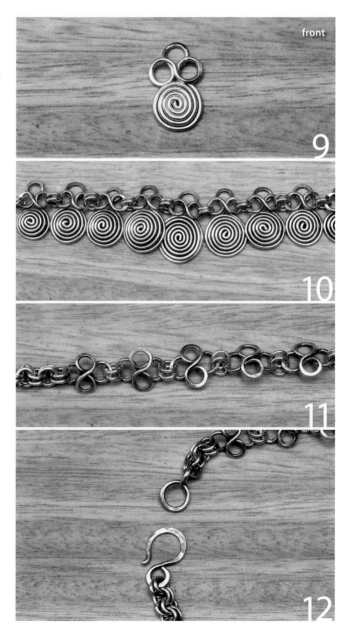

Wire Weaving

Weaving transforms a long strand of wire into a beatiful textile. Woven wire can take on many different appearances and be used in a variety of ways. You can create a woven cord that shines as a central design element, or you can use wire to weave diverse elements into a single piece. The texture and depth of designs is what makes this technique so alluring. Novice wire weavers may find it a challenge to weave long lengths of wire without creating kinks or tangles, but be patient. With a little practice you'll discover the tricks to keeping the wires neat and straight.

Ring of wire

Weaving wire through lengths of chain and then finishing with a flat stone will result in an unusual, any-day ring.

by Kriss Silva

You may think making a ring is beyond your abilities, but this simple wire-and-chain technique will change your mind. Weaving wire through the links of several lengths of chain forms one substantial ring. It can seem more casual or masculine by using thicker chain with 24-gauge wire, or it can become delicate and sophisticated by using finer chain and 26-gauge wire. The project is an excellent starting point for those new to wirework.

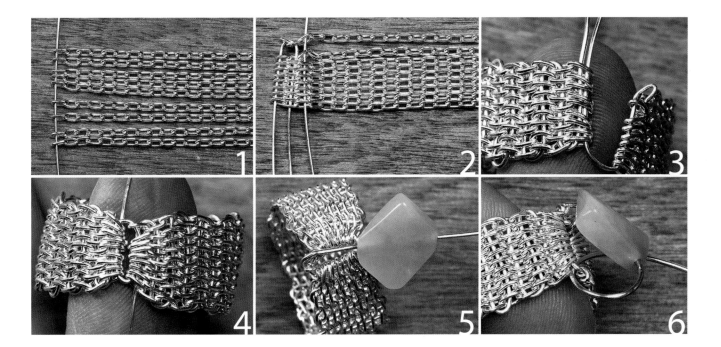

Determine the width and cut the chain.
This ring works best as a wide band; if it's too narrow, it's too flexible and doesn't maintain its shape. The heft of the chain you use will affect the width of the ring. Wrap a length of chain around the finger on which you will wear the ring; count the number of wraps needed for the desired width.

Slide one end of the 24- or 26-gauge wire through one end-link of the chain.
Using the wire as a start point, measure 3 inches (7.6cm) along the length of chain and cut at that mark. Slide the next end-link onto the wire beside the first and cut the chain at the same length. (This is easier if the wire is held horizontally in front of you, with the links smoothed flat.) Continue adding on lengths of chain until the number of chain segments you need for the width of your ring are cut [1].

Weave the wire through the links. Slide the chain segments to one end of the wire, leaving about a 2-inch (5.1cm) tail. Make a curve just beyond the chain segment farthest from the tail, and then weave the long wire end back through the next row of chain links (going in the opposite direction). Keeping the chains

close together, continue to weave the wire back and forth through each row of chain links [2]. To avoid slack in the wire along the outer edges, tighten the wire by hand or with a bentnose pliers after every pass.

Continue weaving until the ring is the desired size, making sure the ending wire tail is on the opposite side as the tail at the beginning. Cut away any excess chain links, if necessary.

Join the ends. One at a time, weave the wire tails through the chain links opposite them to join the two ends [3–4]. Wrap the wire ends around the wire connections, so that each wire is wrapped around the other at both top and bottom of the join. Cut the wires.

Add the stone. Cut a 6-inch (15.2cm) length of 22-gauge wire. Use your pliers to wrap one end around the top connector section of the ring; make a few wraps. Slide the stone on the wire, adjusting the wire to allow for the thickness of the stone [5]. Wrap the wire around the bottom connection section, making a few wraps [6]. Cut the wire and tuck in the cut end with your pliers.

materials

- 1–3 feet (30.5–91.4cm) sterling silver cable chain
- 1 yard (91.4cm) 24- or 26-gauge sterling silver wire
- 6 inches (15.2cm) 22-gauge sterling silver wire
- flat gemstone, same width as finished ring

tools and supplies

- liver of sulfur (optional)
- wire cutters
- chainnose or bentnose pliers
- roundnose pliers

Caged-bead pendant

Anything goes in freeform weaving – just be sure 28-gauge wire will fit through all your bead choices.

by Kate Ferrant Richbourg

Beads proliferate. Leftovers, irresistible single-purchase strands, projects that lost their appeal before they made it all the way to assembly – whatever their stories, loose beads multiply. Scooping up an assortment initiates designer's playtime. Freeform weaving is a fun and creative method for corraling loose beads. These pendants can be simply strung on leather cord, attached to a chain, or built into a dazzling necklace. Start by selecting center-piece nuggets – any larger faceted type will do – then add shapes and sizes to enhance your choice.

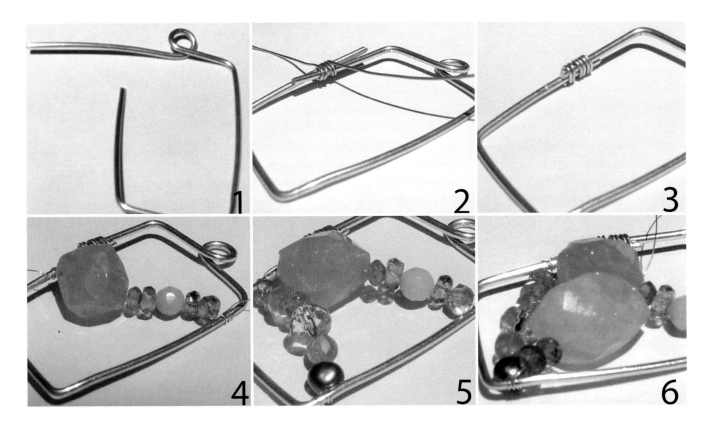

Make the armature. Outline a shape you like on a piece of white paper with a heavy black marker. This drawing will become your template for the armature. The sample is a rectangle measuring ½ inch x 2 inches (13mm x 51mm). A loop at the top allows the pendant to be suspended from a jump ring or bail. Use flatnose pliers to bend the 16-gauge wire to fit the shape of your pattern template [1]. Overlap the ends of the wire in the center of one of the sides or at the bottom of the armature. Wrap the open ends of the armature together with 22-gauge wire to close the shape [2]. Tightly squeeze the ends of the wire wrap around the armature to secure it [3]. Trim the ends.

Wire beads to armature. Cut 12 inches (30.5cm) of 28-gauge wire. Bend the wire in half over the side of the armature; make a few wraps with one end to secure the wire to the armature. Slide a nugget and smaller beads on one wire until they reach the opposite top corner. Wrap the wire around the armature a few times, creating a "spoke" across the armature [4]. Do not cut the wire. Add beads to the other wire end until the beads reach the opposite lower corner, and secure as before, creating a second spoke [5]. Add a third beaded spoke with one of the wires in the same manner [6]. These three spokes will serve as the base.

Fill every space. Continue weaving new beads onto the armature using both wire ends. Use single or multiple beads as needed. If you run out of wire, secure the end inside a bundle of beads, making three wraps in the same place before you cut away the extra wire. Wrap a fresh piece of wire several times to secure it inside a bundle of beads, then continue to weave. If your pendant does not feel solid enough, weave more wire in and around the beads to expand the base. Fill in until no open spaces remain. Add beads around the side of the armature to provide texture and interest.

materials
- sterling silver wire
  - 12 inches (30.5cm) 16-gauge
  - 5 inches (12.7cm) 22-gauge
  - 5–10 feet (1.5–3m) 28-gauge
- 2 semiprecious nugget beads
- assortment of semiprecious beads

tools and supplies
- chainnose pliers
- flatnose pliers
- nylon-jaw pliers
- roundnose pliers
- wire cutters
- ruler or tape measure
- paper
- pen

Woven wire & stone

Stone beads take center stage when they're embellished with a woven wire bezel.

by Kriss Silva

S howcase your wireworking skills by surrounding stone beads with a stunning herringbone wire-weave pattern. This clever wire-weaving technique decoratively frames the stones; the result is a transforming combination of color and texture. To create an interesting choker-length necklace, link together your herringbone bracelet with a coordinating strand and add a large stone surrounded by a herringbone weave to the jump ring on the clasp.

Make the wrapped-loop units. Cut a 12-inch (30.5cm) piece of 24-gauge wire, hold one end with chainnose pliers, and pull the wire through the jaws of your nylon-jaw pliers to straighten it. (If using smaller beads, use 26-gauge wire.) Make a right-angle bend in the wire 1½ inches (38mm) from one end and make the first part of a wrapped loop. Slide the soldered jump ring onto the loop. Complete the wrapped loop, forming 6–8 wraps **[1]**. Trim the excess wrapping wire. Slide a bead on the wire.

Rest the jaws of the chainnose pliers over the wraps, having one edge of the pliers against the loop and the other edge flush with the final wrap. Mark this spot on your pliers with a pen or painter's tape for consistency throughout the project. Make

the first half of a wrapped loop at the other end, parallel to the first loop, using the mark on the pliers as your guide for where to start the loop. Slide a soldered jump ring on the loop, then finish wrapping, ending with the wire perpendicular to the loop **[2]**. The bead should be equal distance from each loop, since you measured the distance with your pliers. Don't cut the wire.

Make the first round of herringbone weave. Bring the wire along the side of the bead, then over and around the wrapped section on the opposite end **[3]**. Bring the wire along the other side of the bead and over and around the wrapped section at this end **[4]**.

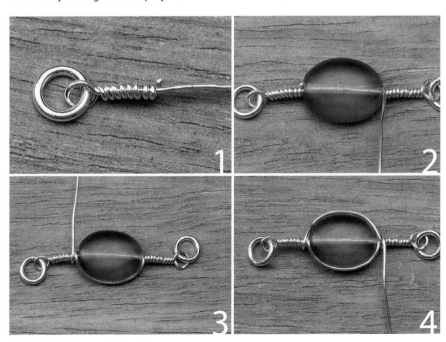

tips
for wrapping wire

For each concentric path around a bead in the herringbone pattern, you need two wire wraps on the neck of the wire. This means that six wraps will allow for three times around a bead, and eight will allow for four times around a bead.

If you want a denser herringbone frame with more wire paths surrounding a bead, make additional wraps around the core wire, keeping the number even. You may need more than 12 inches of wire, depending on the size of the bead and how many wraps you desire.

Wraps are easier to make when the wire core is held firm. After you have made three wraps, reposition your pliers to grasp the wraps, rather than the loop. By gripping the wraps, subsequent wraps are easier to form because you have more leverage and control.

Make the subsequent rounds. Bring the wire along the sides of the bead again, situating this round below the first **[5]**. Wrap the wire around the wrapped ends as before – subsequent rounds will be closer to the loops on each end. Once the desired number of rounds is in place or when the wraps are flush against the loops, wrap around the wrapped core twice, cut the excess wire, and tuck in the end **[6]**.

Join and make the next unit. Make the first half of the wrapped loop for the next unit as before, and link it through the soldered jump ring on one end of the previous unit **[7]**. Continue as before, adding a jump ring to the loop on the opposite end. Use the guide on your pliers to make your wrapped ends the same length. Continue until the bracelet is one unit short of the desired length.

Add the final unit and clasp. Link the first end of the final unit to the previous unit as before. Make the first half of the wrapped loop on the other end and slide a lobster claw clasp on that loop before completing the wraps. Finish the unit as before.

How to determine length

The herringbone weave can be applied to bracelets and necklaces and may be tailored to specific size beads and varying numbers of wraps. Check the chart below for the size bead and number of wraps you desire to determine the length of your project. If what you want isn't listed, make a sample unit, measure it, and substitute it in the most appropriate line below. Multiply the length of this unit by the number listed in the "number of units" column and take into account the diameter of the jump ring. This will give you a preliminary length less the length of your clasp. Your places for adjustments are in the number of wraps (minimal change), jump ring diameter and bead size (small changes), and number of units (significant change).

(length of unit X number of units)
+ [(number of units – 1) X (jump ring diameter in mm ÷ 25.4)]
= bracelet/necklace length less clasp (in inches)

Using the first example below:

(.75" X 7) =		5.25"
[(7 – 1 = 6) X (5mm ÷ 25.4 = .197")] =	+	1.18"
	=	6.43"

	Bead size	Number of wraps (24-gauge wire)	Approximate length of unit	Number of units	Jump ring diameter	Preliminary length less clasp
Bracelets	6mm	4	.75"	7	5mm	6.43"
	6mm	4	.75"	8	5mm	7.18"
	6mm	4	.75"	8	8mm	8.21"
	8mm	3	.81"	7	6mm	7.09"
	9mm	4	.88"	7	5mm	7.34"
	10mm	4	1.00"	7	4mm	7.94"
	11mm	5	1.13"	6	7mm	8.16"
Necklaces	8mm	3	.81"	17	6mm	17.55"
	8mm	3	.81"	18	6mm	18.59"
	8mm	3	.81"	18	5mm	17.93"
	9mm	4	.88"	15	5mm	15.96"
	9mm	4	.88"	15	6mm	16.50"

Conversely, let's say you know you want to make a 17-inch (43.2cm) necklace. You have your lobster claw clasp and soldered jump ring, and together they add up to ¾ inch (.75"/19mm). Subtract the length of the clasp from the desired length (17" – .75" = 16.25"). You made a sample unit; it measured about ⅞ inch (.88"/22mm) long. You like the proportion of 5mm jump rings with your herringbone units, so let's plug those in using the formula from above and the appropriate line under necklaces in the chart.

(.88" X 15) =		13.2"
[(15 – 1 = 14)] X (5mm ÷ 25.4 = .197")] =	+	2.75"
	=	15.95"

A little short, but if you add a 4mm jump ring between the clasp sections and the first and last units, the necklace would measure 16.25 inches; finished with the lobster claw clasp and soldered jump ring, it will be 17 inches total.

materials

- 2–4 yards (1.8–3.7m) of 24-gauge dead-soft wire
- 6–10 beads, 6–11mm in length
- 5–9 soldered jump rings
- lobster claw clasp and soldered jump ring

tools and supplies

- flush cutters
- ruler
- bentnose pliers
- chainnose pliers
- nylon-jaw pliers
- roundnose pliers
- pen or painter's tape

Viking
splendor

An ancient weaving technique produces spectacular modern jewelry.

by Kate Ferrant Richbourg & Anne Mitchell

Wire weaving – knitting fine strands of metal into a meshlike chain – dates to the Vikings. A basic technique, wire weaving can be modified easily to produce dramatic results. This project introduces two types of weaving. Single weave gets the chain started and may be used for the entire length, creating an open, airy weave that's quick to stitch. Double weave, which involves backtracking two rows onto a single weave, creates a denser, more compact link. (For a very dense mesh, try a triple weave; simply backtrack three rows instead of two.) Drawing the finished knit strand through a wooden drawplate hardens the wire, tightens the weaving, and shapes and sizes the chain.

Once you've mastered the basics, experiment with different dowel and wire sizes, change the number of starting loops, or work in mixed types of wire, such as copper and silver; you can also patinate the final chain. Whether you weave chain to showcase a beautiful hand-blown bead or as a tribute to an ancient art form, you'll be delighted with the range of styles you can create.

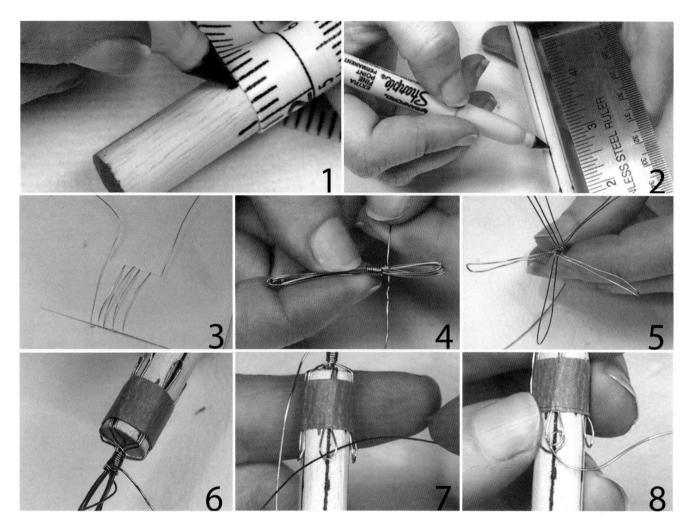

Prepare the dowel. Make five evenly spaced marks around the end of a dowel **[1]**. (The marks are just under 3/16 inch/5mm apart on a 3/8 -inch/9.5mm dowel.) Draw straight lines down the dowel to guide the wire-loop placement **[2]**.

Set up the weave. Wrap 24-gauge copper wire around the cardstock five times. Leave a long tail on one end and a short tail on the other **[3]**. Slip the wire off the cardstock. Use the short wire tail to bind the loops together at one end to form a bundle **[4]**. The remaining long wire will be used to begin the weave. Spread the loops of the bundle equally to form a daisy **[5]**. Place the daisy over the end of the dowel and bend the loops down. Align each loop with a line on the dowel. Secure the daisy with masking tape **[6]**. (Do not catch the long piece of wire under the tape.)

Begin the chain with single weave. Hold the dowel in your nondominant hand. Beginning with any loop of the daisy, use your dominant hand to pass the long piece of wire under the right side of the starting loop and out through the center **[7]**. The wire should form a loop that links into the starting loop **[8]**. Repeat with each of the other four loops to make the first row, working in a clockwise direction **[9]**. Keep

materials

- sterling silver wire:
  - 48 feet (14.6m) 24-gauge, dead-soft
  - 1 foot (30.5cm) 22-gauge, dead-soft
- 3 feet (91.4cm) 24-gauge, dead-soft, copper wire
- pair of end caps
- slider beads or pendant (optional)
- two 3mm round beads
- clasp and soldered jump ring

tools and supplies

- 3/8-inch-diameter (9.5mm) wood dowel, 12 inches (30.5cm) long
- fine-point permanent marker
- tape measure
- ruler
- masking tape
- cardstock, 1½ x 3 inches (3.8 x 7.6cm)
- chainnose pliers
- roundnose pliers
- nylon-jaw pliers
- flush cutters
- draw plate
- bench vise

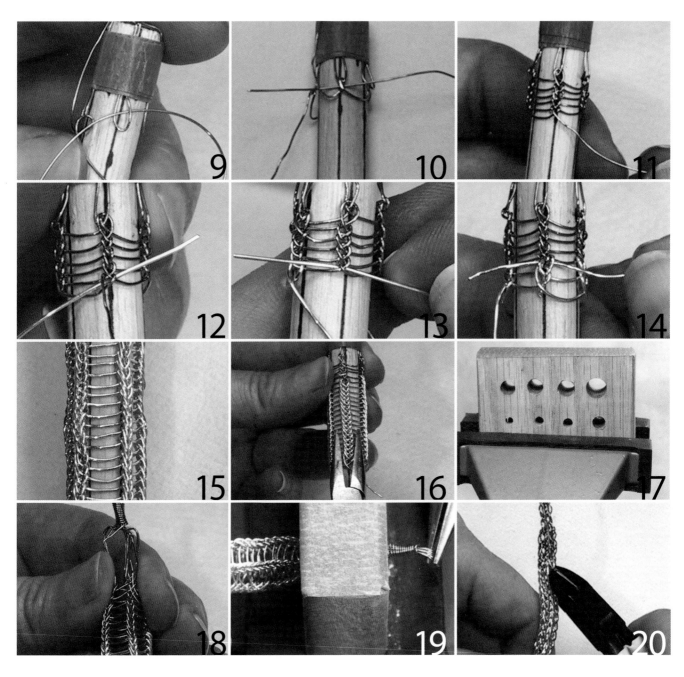

the rows straight by lining up the cross of each loop with a mark on the dowel. To make the second row, and all the following rows, look at the first loop you made. Below the loop there should be an "X" where the wire crosses over itself. Pass the long piece of wire (from the right) behind the X [10]. Do not pass it through the loop. Repeat until six continuous copper-wire rows are complete [11].

Join a new wire. Cut 2 feet (61cm) of silver wire. Lay the end of the copper wire along the dowel. To join the new wire, pass the silver wire from the left to the right under the X of the current loop and bend

it so it lies next to the copper wire [12]. (These two ends may be cut away after several new rows are woven; the ends will be caught inside the chain when you run it through the draw plate.) Repeat the single-weave technique with the silver wire [13]. Use this technique each time you need to add a new piece of wire. Use the new piece of silver wire to weave a few more rows.

Continue the chain with double weave. Count back two rows and slide the wire under the X of the next loop in sequence [14]. Continue to double weave around the dowel until the chain is 20 percent shorter than your desired finished

length [15]. If your rows become uneven, pinch them slightly with your chainnose pliers to keep them straight [16]. As soon as the weave feels stable, undo the tape and push the top part of the chain up and off the dowel. Always keep only an inch or two of dowel inside the chain to stabilize it while you are weaving. If you leave more of the dowel in the chain, it will stick and be difficult to remove.

Shape the chain. Secure the draw plate in a vise [17]. Pinch the copper end of the chain together so it will fit in the first hole of the draw plate [18]. Push the end of the chain into the largest hole in the draw-

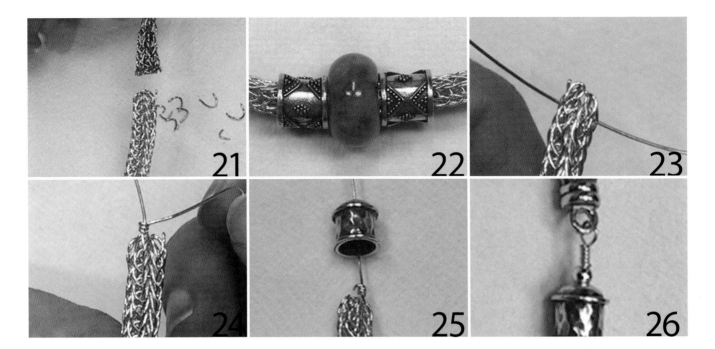

plate. Grab the bundle with flatnose or chainnose pliers and pull it through the hole **[19]** (this is a top-down view). Determine the desired diameter of the chain, based on the size of the end caps. Draw the chain through each subsequent hole in the draw plate until the chain is the desired diameter. Cut away the starting bundle and any uneven rows of weaving at the beginning of the chain **[20–21]**.

Finish the necklace. String beads or a pendant on the chain, if desired **[22]**. Cut two 6-inch (15.2cm) pieces of 22-gauge wire. Thread one piece through the end of the chain **[23]**. Make a tight wrap over the top of the chain to secure it **[24]**. Trim the short end. Thread the end cap over the remaining end of the wire **[25]**. String a 3mm bead and make the first half of a wrapped loop. Add the clasp and complete the wraps **[26]**. Repeat on the other end of the chain with the second 6-inch wire, the second end cap, and the soldered jump ring.

tips on
weaving wire

Weaving is a rhythmic process and, once learned, practically occurs without volition. Here are a few pointers to get you to that stage:

- The wire daisy you create at the beginning is the key to the size of your chain. Each wrap around the cardstock becomes one loop of the starting petal for the chain. A five-loop chain needs five wraps around the cardstock. Vary the look of your chain by changing the number of loops.

- Practice weaving chain with inexpensive copper wire to perfect your technique.

- Straighten your wire by placing it in a folded polishing cloth and drawing it through nylon-jaw pliers. You may need to straighten the wire again as you weave.

- Use a larger or smaller dowel to alter the look of your finished chain; a large dowel will create a softer, airier woven tube, while a smaller dowel will produce a tighter, heftier tube.

- The starter part of the chain is cut away after the chain is pulled through the draw plate. The loops in the weave may be either tight or loose; what's important is whether the spaces between them are even. Don't fret over a few uneven patches. Many mistakes will be smoothed over when the chain is pulled through the draw plate.

- As you become a more proficient weaver, you may wish to work with longer lengths of wire so there are fewer joins in the chain.

Bezels and Frames

Using metal to frame a gemstone or focal piece is an ancient tradition, but modern wire jewelry artists are finding new and exciting ways to create the look of a traditional setting. The appeal of this technique isn't just the finely detailed appearance of the finished piece, but also its relative simplicity. A long-held belief has been that only metalworkers with an arsenal of torches and tools can accomplish the types of projects featured in this section, but these wire artists prove this theory wrong.

The art and elegance of these pieces lies in the fact that with just a few materials and basic tools, artists can create detailed, delicate pieces. The minute scale of some pieces provides new challenges and lessons to jewelry makers of all levels looking to expand their skills and add new dimensions to their work.

Captured coin

Use this versatile wire-wrap approach to turn any minted coin into a necklace focal point.

by Anna Lemons

Who hasn't held a beautiful minted coin or commemorative medal and marveled at the artistry it represents? Some coins recall places or milestone years or particular events. Others turn into good-luck charms. Dig those pretty disks out of the drawer. This project provides a way to turn a numismatist's memento into a pendant.

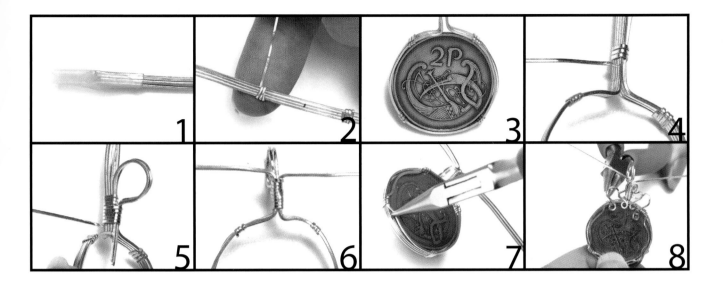

Prepare the wire. Measure the circumference of your coin and add 3 inches (7.6cm). Cut four pieces of square wire to this length. Holding one piece of wire at a time with flatnose pliers, straighten and clean the wire by running it through a polishing cloth. Place the wires side by side. Lightly tape them at the ends so they will stay flat and flush as you work [1]. Mark the midpoint by making tiny dots with your marker on the inner two wires.

Bind wires together. Divide your coin's circumference by four to determine the spacing between your binds. Using your dots as the center point between the two middle binds, mark the placement of all four binds. Cut a 10-inch (25.4cm) length of half-round wire. Use flatnose pliers to make a tiny hook in one end, dome side out. Hook the half-round wire across the four wires at one of the binding marks. Make three tight wraps around the square wires [2]. Nip the end off on the side where you began. Repeat at each binding mark.

Make a bezel. Placing the center point dots at the bottom of your coin, wrap the wire bundle around the coin. Where they meet at the top, bend each bundle of wires upward at a 90-degree angle [3]. Remove the coin from the bezel. Use the half-round binding wire to wrap the eight wires together 3/16 inch (5mm) above the bend [4]. Don't cut the binding wire.

Make a bail. Remove the tape from the bundles. Select the backmost wire from each bundle. Bend the two selected wires around a pen or dowel until the ends point in the direction opposite the ends of other six wires. Leave the starting side of the loop flat where it touches the other six wires. Wrap the uncut binding wire several more times around the ends of the loop and the original six wires [5]. Snip the binding wire. Use flatnose pliers to squeeze the binding wraps tightly together. Cut the two bail wires where they emerge at the bottom of the binds. Divide the remaining wires and bend them at 90-degree angles away from the bail in opposite directions [6].

Secure the coin. Place the coin in the bezel; it should fit snugly. Using flatnose pliers, form small bends to each side of the binds in the top square wire. This will hold the coin in place at the front [7]. Make similar bends in the wire on the other side of the coin to hold the back in place.

Embellish the top. Use roundnose pliers to curl the remaining loose wire ends into loops or other decorative elements, trimming as desired [8], and gently separate the two bail wires into a V-shape using flatnose pliers.

materials

- sterling silver wire:
  - 1 yard (91.4cm) square, 22-gauge, dead-soft
  - 10 inches (25.4cm) half-round, 22-gauge, half-hard
- coin or medal

tools and supplies

- tape measure
- tape
- fine-tip permanent marker
- flatnose pliers
- roundnose pliers
- wire cutters
- pen or dowel
- polishing cloth

Simple elegance

Square and half-round wire form a sophisticated bezel and bail for a triangular cabochon.

by Anna Lemons

Although wirework often takes on the feeling of filigree, the clean lines of this glass cabochon beg for a different treatment. Using a square-wire framework keeps this design simple and exposes much of the glass. The modern angularity of this wrap and the sleek treatment of the bail finish the almost–Art Deco look.

Prepare the wire. Measure the perimeter of your cabochon and add 3 inches (7.6cm) to that measurement. (The cabochon shown has three 1-inch-long/25.5mm sides; adding 3 inches to that measurement gives a total of 6 inches/15.2cm.) With flush cutters, cut four pieces of square wire to that length. Holding one piece of wire at a time with a flatnose pliers, straighten and clean the wire by running it between two layers of the polishing cloth. Place the wires side by side. Lightly tape them at the ends so they will stay flush and flat as you work. Mark the midpoint by making a tiny dot on the inner wires **[1]**.

Bind the wires together. Determine where you want to place your binds by measuring the cabochon. (For this cabochon, the first binds were placed ³⁄₁₆ inch/5mm from the center mark. The second binds were placed ⁵⁄₈ inch/16mm from the first.) Translate the bind placements onto the square wire with a pen or marker. Cut a 6-inch length of half-round wire. Use flatnose pliers to make a tiny hook at one end, dome-side out. Hook the half-round wire across the four square wires at one of the binding marks. Make three tight wraps around the square wires **[2]**. Nip the end off on the same side where you began. Repeat at each mark.

Shape the bezel. Wrap the wire bundle around the cabochon, using flatnose pliers to make sharp, even angles **[3]**. Where they

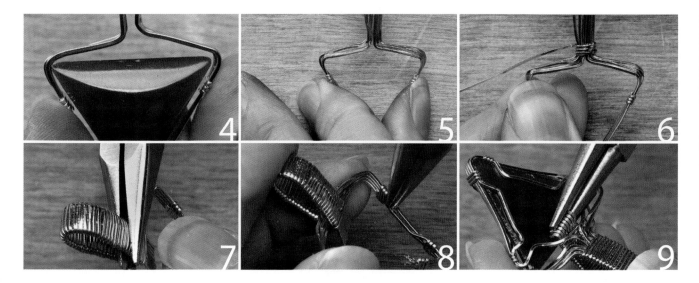

will meet at the top, bend each bundle so the ends stick straight up at the center top of the cabochon **[4]**.

Prepare the bail. Remove the tape from the end of the wires. Fan and flatten the eight wires with the pliers **[5]**.

Wrap the bail. Cut a 28-inch (71.1cm) piece of half-round wire. Keeping the square wires flush and flat, bind them together with half-round wire, dome-side out, making a small hook to start. Starting closest to the cabochon, keep the wraps parallel and do not overlap **[6]**; work toward the ends of the wire, ending about ¼ inch (6.5mm) from the end of the shortest wire. Cut the eight square wires even with the shortest one. Cut the binding wire. Use flatnose pliers to press the binds flat. File the ends of the square wires to remove any burs or sharp edges.

Form the bail. Bend the eight bound wires around a pen or small dowel, towards the front of the pendant. Use your flatnose pliers to align the bail **[7]**.

Secure the cabochon. Place the cabochon in the bezel to check the fit. Remove it. Using flatnose pliers, form small bends on the front of the bezel beside each side-bind **[8]**. Slide the cabochon in place from the top. Form similar bends behind the cabochon to keep it in the bezel. Make additional bends to the wire across the top of the bezel on front and back to finish securing the cabochon. Shake the piece; the cabochon should be wrapped snugly and shouldn't rattle.

Finish the ends. Using roundnose pliers, curve the ¼-inch tails toward the back side of the cabochon so they don't snag fabric or scratch skin **[9]**.

materials
- gold-filled wire:
  - 24 inches (61cm) square, 22-gauge, dead-soft
  - 52 inches (1.3m) half-round, 22-gauge, half-hard
- triangular-shaped glass cabochon

tools and supplies
- ruler
- flush cutters
- chainnose or flatnose pliers
- roundnose pliers
- polishing cloth
- tape
- pen or fine-point marker
- file

Bound beauty

This stunning and sophisticated wirework ring
will entangle you in its charms.

by Angel Ortiz

The sweeping wirework of this ring creates an open yet sturdy setting for almost any elongated stone. In the artist's version, an 18x9mm marquise-cut smoky quartz perches snugly between the lines, adding extra radiance to the curvaceous wire loops. (A 32x15mm pink agate is used in the process photos.) Though the wires of this delicate ring intertwine, overlap, and entangle with one another, the technique is surprisingly uncomplicated.

Prepare the wire. Cut eight 4½-inch (11.4cm) pieces of 20-gauge square wire. Rub and straighten the wire with a polishing cloth. Line up the wires on a flat surface parallel to each other and tape the ends together on each side. This will keep the wire flush and flat as you work. Place a mark in the center of the wires. Then measure ¾ inch (19mm) from each side of the mark, and mark those two places **[1]**.

Bind the wires. Cut approximately 6 inches (15.2cm) of half-round wire. File one end of the wire and form a small hook. Place this hook on one of the outer marks. Begin binding the square wires with the half-round wire, working toward the taped edge; make sure the flat side of the half-round wire is against the square wires. Make six wraps. Begin and end on the same side. Repeat this procedure at the other outer mark **[2]**.

Shape using a mandrel. Using the center mark, place the wire bundle on a ring mandrel **[3]**. The shank of the mandrel should be set one size smaller than the ring size you would like to make. With the binding ends facedown (the underside of the ring), press down on both bindings, making a horseshoe shape **[4]**. Remove the shank and look at the ring to make sure the bindings are centered and straight. Then move the shank three sizes down on the mandrel and press down on the bindings again.

Create prong settings. Using a butter knife (or any knife without serrated edges), spread open the first wire and bend it down toward the taped ends **[5]**. Then spread the second wire and bend it down to approximately an 80-degree angle **[6]**. These will be your upper and lower prongs. Repeat on the opposite side **[7]**.

Holding the ring with the U-shaped side facing you, use the tip of a chainnose pliers to create an area for your stone to be set. Slightly flatten the center of one of your upper prongs using the tip of the pliers (these loops are initially very rounded). Then place the pliers on the center of the lower prong and push down, making the lower prong slightly flatter also **[8]**. Repeat these steps on the opposite side.

Mount the stone. Position the stone in the center of the prongs **[9]**. The easiest way is to gently move the wires close together with your fingers and push the stone in the setting. Lightly pinch the wires together with your fingers. This type of tension setting helps secure the stone.

Wrap the wire. Hold the ring with one side of the U shape facing you, then bend an outermost wire down from each side and parallel to the shank **[10]**. Cross the wires over the shank to form an X shape **[11]**. Wrap the wire that is closest to the shank underneath and cut it. Wrap the wire that forms the top of the X shape under-

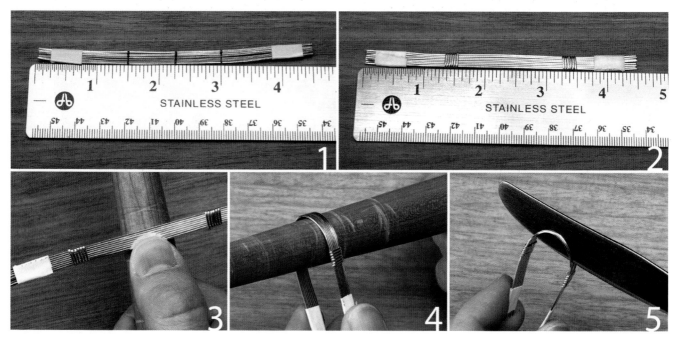

neath and bring it around to the top, forming a straight line under the X **[12]**. This line is the starting point for wrapping the shank, as it provides a nice guide for an even bind. Repeat on the opposite side. Using a small, flat, jeweler's file, sand the cut ends until they are smooth. Take your time wrapping the wire, being careful not to mar it. If you do nick the wire, use the file to smooth it.

Finish the wraps. Bend the next outermost wires down to the lower prong and tuck the ends underneath (bend one from the left side and one from the right side) **[13]**. Do this with the remaining wires, and repeat the process on the opposite side. Keep these wires neat, close, and even as you bend them. For an optional touch, twist the last two remaining wires – one on each side – using a pin vise and wrap them underneath **[14]**.

Wrap the shank of ring. Wrap the shank of your ring using 20-gauge half-round wire.

tips on retaining shape

When bending and twisting the wire to create the sides of the ring, keep a finger or thumb on the band to make sure the wires aren't overlapping. It's easy to focus on the side embellishments and forget to maintain the shape of the band. If you like, you can wrap the band with plastic-coated wire to hold the shape while you work.

materials
- sterling silver wire:
  - 1 yard (91.4cm) square, 20-gauge, half-hard
  - 12 inches (30.5cm) half-round, 20-gauge, half-hard
- marquise-cut stone

tools and supplies
- ruler
- flush cutters
- polishing cloth
- masking tape
- marker
- ring mandrel
- butter knife
- chainnose pliers
- flat jeweler's file
- pin vise (optional)
- plastic-coated wire (optional)

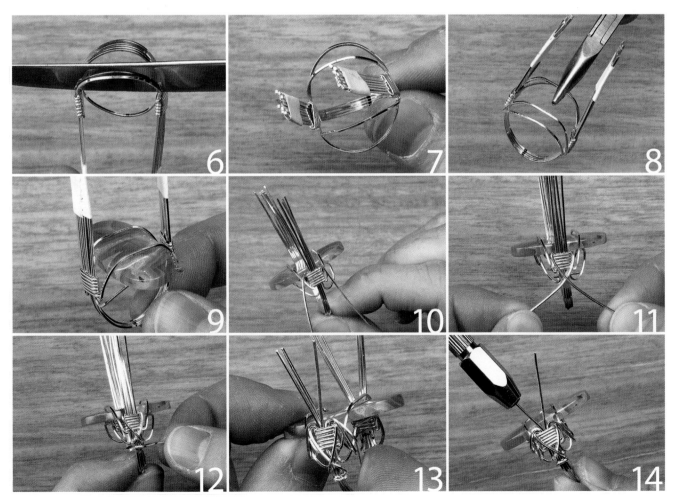

Silver stream

*Silver wire and sponge coral pair up in this attractive
bracelet and pendant set.*

by Angel Ortiz & Joanne Ortiz

G racefully flowing silver wire streams around coral beads like water over pebbles in this duo. Made with only silver wire, beads, and an optional silver centerpiece, the techniques used for shaping the wire are what take center stage. The clean, clear lines of wire are interrupted by colorful pieces of sponge coral; a simple clasp design gives the bracelet a straightforward elegance. The pendant is draped with strands of spiraled silver wire – the perfect companion to accompany the bracelet.

Bracelet

Prepare the wire. Cut the following quantities and lengths of 20-gauge square wire: one 16½-inch (41.9cm) piece, five 8-inch (20.3cm) pieces, one 3½-inch (8.9cm) piece, and one 6-inch (15.2cm) piece. Cut the following quantities and lengths of 20-gauge half-round wire: two 6-inch (15.2cm) pieces and four 3-inch (7.6cm) pieces. Straighten and clean the wire pieces using a polishing cloth.

Bind the wire bundle. Find the center of the 16½-inch (41.9cm) wire and bend it in half. Line up the five 8-inch (20.3cm) pieces of wire in between the two legs, which are now your outer wires. Wrap masking tape around the loop end of the wire bundle to help keep the wires straight [1].

Measure ¼ inch (6.5mm) in from the loop end and mark this spot across the wires. Make a small hook at the end of a 6-inch (15.2cm) piece of half-round wire, place the hook on the mark, and make six wraps around the wire bundle, moving toward the center as you wrap. Once you've made six wraps, cut the wire and tuck the end underneath. The cut ends are positioned on the back of your work [2].

Use flatnose or chainnose pliers to grasp the five wires that are in between the looped wire. Bend these wires back onto the wrapped binding that you just made, creating a hook. Press the edge of this hook down onto the binding [3].

Twist selected wires (optional). For added character, you can choose to twist the two outermost wires or the center wire that will run through the center of the beads. Twisting is done using a pin vise. If you choose to do this, be sure to use flatnose or chainnose pliers to secure the binding while twisting to prevent any unwanted twisting elsewhere [4].

Add a second binding. Measure 1 inch (2.5cm) from the end of the first binding and make a mark. Create a three-wrap binding at this mark using a 3-inch (7.6cm) piece of half-round wire. Cut and tuck the end neatly underneath [5].

Add a small coral bead and third binding. With the wires that are extending out from the binding, bend the three outermost wires from each side out at 45-degree angles. Run the remaining center wire through an 8mm sponge coral bead, pushing the bead as close to the base as possible [6].

Grasp one of the three-wire bundles with your hand, and form it evenly around the bead. Now grasp the three wires with flatnose or chainnose pliers so that the tip of the pliers is positioned across the area where you would like to create a bend [7]. Bend all three wires at a 90-degree angle so they are parallel with the center wire [8]. Repeat on the other side. Bring all wires together on the other side of the bead and make a three-wrap binding around them [9].

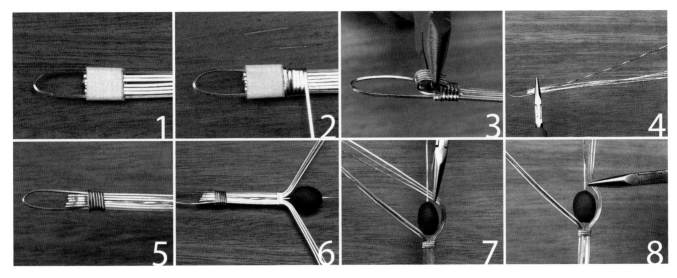

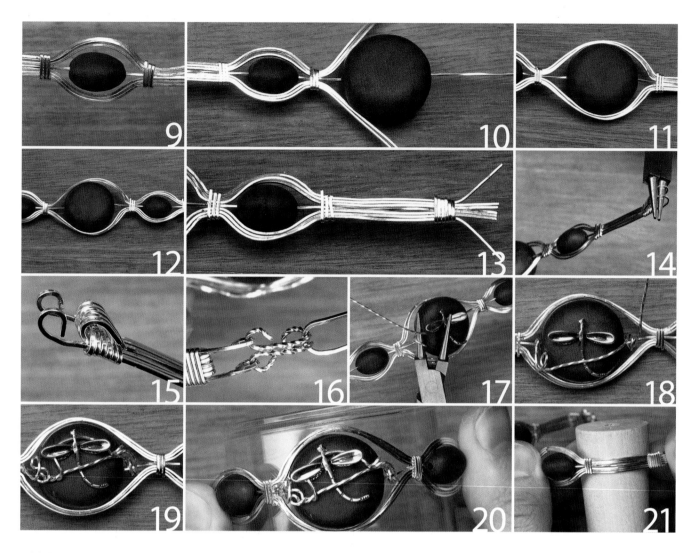

Add the center bead and fourth binding.
Using the process from the previous step,
slide the 20mm bead onto the center wire
and form the wires around it on each side
[10]. Make a three-wrap binding on the
other side of the center bead **[11]**.

Add a small bead and fifth binding.
Slide an 8mm bead onto the center wire,
form the wires around it on each side, and
make another three-wrap binding **[12]**.

Add the final binding. Place a mark
1 inch (2.5cm) from the previous binding.
Create a six-wrap binding at this mark **[13]**.
Use chainnose pliers to bend the five
center wires back into a hook shape, as
done on the other side of the bracelet. Cut
these wires flush. Press the hook down
onto the wraps. Leave the two outermost
wires extended out.

Create the clasp. Cut the outer two wires
even with one another. Use roundnose

pliers to form the wires into hooks **[14–15]**.
Cut a 3½-inch (8.9cm) piece of 20-gauge
square wire and twist it with a pin vise.
Fold it in half using roundnose pliers,
and then make a small hook with the
loop end. With the two free ends, form
two loops facing outward. Attach these
loops to the hooks **[16]**.

**Add embellishments to the center bead
(optional).** Determine which side of bead
to use for the front. Apply epoxy or
cement to the backside of a sterling silver
charm (in this project, a dragonfly), let it sit
for about a minute, and secure it on top of
the center of the bead. (Cement usually
takes about 24 hours to fully cure, but will
decently hold after 30 minutes.) Align the
parts of the charm that stick out most with
the holes of the bead (for example, the
dragonfly wings).

Twist a 6-inch (15.2cm) piece of square
wire, make a small hook at one end, and
secure the hook to the wire that goes

through the center of the 20mm bead.
Tighten it with pliers if necessary. Spiral the
wire around roundnose pliers for decoration **[17]**, bring the wire across the charm,
and wrap the wire around the center wire
at the other side of the bead **[18]**. Create
more spirals and then bring the wire in
between the wings and under the head of
the dragonfly. Loop the wire underneath
the spirals on the side you began on, cut it,
and tuck in the end. Make sure the wire is
wrapped snugly to prevent movement of
the silver piece **[19]**. You may need to
improvise to attach your metal embellishment. This part of the project is best done
free-form – bending and shaping the wire
attractively to secure the silver element as
best you can.

Shape the bracelet. Use a bracelet
mandrel for shaping. If not available, use
any curved household item (a hard plastic
cup was used for the bracelet shown).
Position the center of the bracelet on the

mandrel or curved object, and press down on both wraps next to the center bead [20]. Then use the larger portion of a ring mandrel (or a curved item smaller than the previous) to shape each side of the bracelet, pressing downward to get a slightly rounded shape [21]. Adjust as needed by hand. Close the clasp, and you're finished!

Pendant

Prepare the wire and string the bead.
Straighten 12 inches (30.5cm) of 20-gauge square wire with a polishing cloth. Make a coil at the end of the length of wire using roundnose and chainnose pliers, and slide the wire up through the 20mm bead until the wire coil is flush against the bottom of the bead [1].

Create a wire loop. Using roundnose pliers, make a loop close to the bead. Keeping the pliers in the loop, wrap the tail of the wire around the stem once or twice right above the bead [2]. Remove the pliers. Bring the excess wire to the front of your pendant. For added interest, you can twist this remaining wire with a pin vise if you like.

Add a silver element to the pendant bead. Apply epoxy or cement to the back of the dragonfly charm or silver embellishment of your choice. Let it sit for about 1 minute and then secure the charm on the center bead. (Cement usually takes 24 hours to fully cure but should hold after 30 minutes.)

Secure the wire over your silver element. This part of the project is best done free-form – bending and shaping the wire attractively to secure the silver element as best you can.

Bend the wire down and into a swooping S-shape that crosses over your metal charm (a dragonfly wing in this example), and then travels down and crosses your charm in a second area (here, the dragonfly tail). Bring the wire down to the bottom of the pendant and make one or two loops around the stem of the coil [3]. Add a few spirals in the wire using roundnose pliers, and then bend the wire back up toward the top of the pendant and cross your metal element in another place (the other dragonfly wing).

With the remaining wire, make some loops around the stem of the top wire loop [4]. Cut the tail to approximately ¾ inch (19mm), form a coil, and press the coil down near the base of the wire loop [5].

Attach a bail to the wire loop. Open the bail, attach it to the wire loop, and close the bail [6]. Slide a chain of your choice through the bail, and you're done!

materials

bracelet
- sterling silver wire:
  - 66 inches (1.7m) square, 20-gauge, half-hard
  - 24 inches (61cm) half-round, 20-gauge, half-hard
- 20mm round bead
- 2 8–10mm round beads
- sterling silver charm

pendant
- 12 inches (30.5cm) square, 20-gauge, sterling silver wire, half-hard
- 20mm round bead
- sterling silver charm
- sterling silver bail

tools and supplies
- ruler
- wire cutters
- polishing cloth
- masking tape
- pin vise (optional)
- marker
- chainnose or flatnose pliers
- roundnose pliers
- nylon-jaw pliers (optional)
- bracelet mandrel or other large curved object
- ring mandrel or other small curved object
- epoxy or cement

Amplified
brilliance

*Wrap a picture-perfect citrine
in a 14k gold-filled wire frame.*

by Anna Lemons

Fine wire wraps embracing a gemstone give this pendant a softness unachievable through other artistic means. Just as water eagerly flows into nooks and crevices in its path, wire can be molded into challenging shapes that other jewelry-making media cannot. Wire's flexibility allows it to caress curves, tuck into minute cracks, and morph into myriad forms.

In this project, you will wrap a tantalizing 14k gold-filled wire bezel around a sparkling brilliant-cut citrine. While you may begin at your workbench with just a few straight lengths of plain wire, you will end up with a piece of pure baroque elegance. This pendant is best suited for artists who are skilled in wireworking.

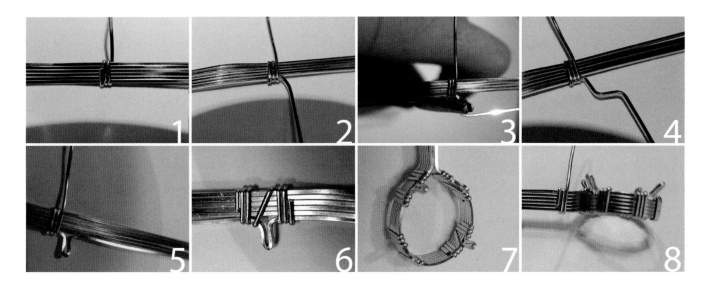

Measure and prepare the wire.
Calculate the length of your wire bundle by measuring your gem's circumference and adding 3 inches (7.6cm) for the bail. In the pendant shown, a 2-inch (5.1cm) circumference plus 3 inches (7.6cm) for the bail equals a total of 5 inches (12.7cm). Now determine the number of wires (placed on top of each other) needed to correspond to the depth of the gem's pavilion – the distance from its girdle to its culet (see "Anatomy of a Gemstone," p. 65). For the 14mm citrine shown, six 5-inch (12.7cm) pieces of square wire were laid beside each other to match the depth of the gem.

After cutting the appropriate number of wires, clean and straighten them by rubbing them with a polishing cloth several times.

Mark prong locations on the gem. Using the gem's circumference measurement, incrementally mark prong placements with a water-soluble marker or pen. In the pendant shown, prongs are placed at 1, 4, 8, and 11 o'clock positions around the gem. You can place the prongs at other positions, provided they are evenly spaced.

Wrap the first prong binding. Lay your wires side by side so they are flush with each other. Starting from the exact center, begin a three-wrap bind using a 5-inch (12.7cm) piece of half-round wire, round-side up. Finish three wraps, but do not cut the tail of the wire [1]; the tail will come into play as you finish the prong.

Shape the prong. Hold the wire bundle horizontally, with the wire tail from the binding extending upward. Use your fingers to grab the bottommost wire in the bundle, on the right side of the binding, and bend it down at a 90-degree angle [2]. On this wire, measure $^{15}/_{64}$ inch (6mm) away from the bundle, grasp this location with flatnose pliers, and bend the wire upward at a 90-degree angle [3]. Measure $^{15}/_{64}$ inch from this second bend and create a third 90-degree angle bend downward. The wire should now resemble a zigzag pattern [4].

Finish the prong. Use flatnose pliers or your fingers to pinch the zigzag shape together and align the rest of the wire so it is parallel with the wires in the bundle [5]. Keep the prong wire flush against the bundle. Use the tail (the wire that is

extending upward) to cross over the back of the bundle and create a three-wrap binding on the other side of the prong [6]. Cut the wire ends and press them both against the inside of the bundle using flatnose pliers.

Continue to make three other prong units exactly like this one; evenly space them along the length of the wire bundle. You may need to create more of these units or allow more space between them, depending on the size and shape of your gemstone.

Form a circular bezel. Use a ring mandrel, marker, or round dowel to form the wire bundle into a circle with the cut ends facing the interior. The size of the bezel should be slightly smaller than the circumference of the gem to hold it securely.

At the closure of the circle, use flatnose pliers to grasp one side of the wire bundle. Bend this side straight up at a 45-degree angle. Repeat with the other side of the wire bundle [7]. Make sure the prongs are evenly spaced and that your bail will be centered. Also, check to see that your gem will sit in this bezel without falling through. Adjust accordingly. Starting at the top and working down, bind the top wire bundles

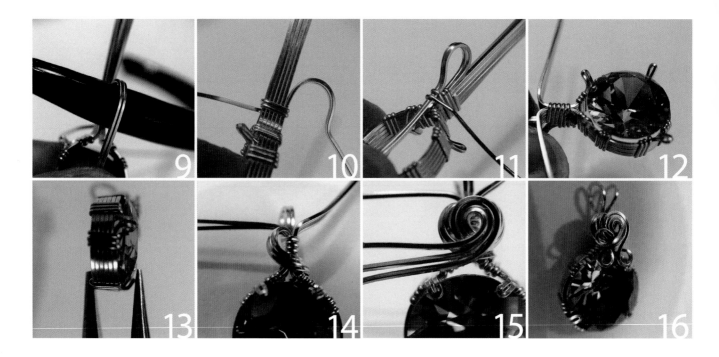

together two to three times using a 6-inch (15.2cm) piece of half-round wire **[8]**. Do not cut the end of this binding wire.

Shape the bail. Hold the bezel with the back facing you. Using the large diameter of a roundnose pliers or the handle of the pliers, form one rounded bend in the two back wires that are facing you **[9]**. Make sure this bail will accommodate your chain. At the base of this curvature, bend the two wires away from the pendant at a 45-degree angle **[10]**. Pinch the base (the 45-degree angle) of these two wires against the back wires of the pendant. Bind them all together with a three-wrap binding using the tail of half-round wire you used to bind the bezel together **[11]**.

Trim the tail of the binding wire and press it down against the side of the binding wraps using flatnose pliers. Also trim the tails of the bail wires and press them down tightly against the binding wraps. This step will anchor the wires securely, ensuring the bail doesn't come apart with wear and tear. Bend the

remaining bundle wires out to either side at 90-degree angles – half to one side, half to the other as shown in photo 12.

Set the gem. Bend your prongs outward slightly and set your gem in place **[12]**. Hold the gem evenly and firmly inside the bezel. Use your roundnose pliers to roll each prong up and over the gem. Don't try for an extremely tight fit just yet. Once all prongs are positioned over the gem, use chainnose pliers to press them down against the gem **[13]**. Slowly apply even pressure to all four sides until the prongs are secured around the gem; the gem shouldn't rock in the bezel.

Add the finishing touches. The remaining wires at the top are used as decoration. In the pendant shown, three wires from the left were brought across the front to the right, trimmed, and tucked beneath the bezel **[14]**. The wires from the right were formed into a loop in the center of the pendant **[15]**, and three tendrils were curled

with roundnose pliers and left hanging down **[16]**.

This step is best done free-form, so visualize a design that is appealing to you and have fun putting the finishing touches on your pendant. Separate the two wires of the bail into an attractive V shape. File any wire ends that could irritate the wearer and smooth any nicks made by your pliers during construction. Then slide the pendant on a chain and enjoy!

color of
wire

Gold wire was chosen for this project to set off the warm tones of the citrine. If you select another gem that has cool tones, such as amethyst or aquamarine, silver wire may be a better choice.

Matching the tone of the wire to the gemstone you are using enhances the clean and elegant appearance of your finished piece. Garnets, rubies, gold topazes, and other "warm" gems will look their best in gold settings, particularly if a traditional effect is desired.

However, don't overlook the opportunity to set a gemstone in a nontraditional fashion with an unexpected choice in metal. You may end up with something spectacular!

materials

- 14k gold-filled wire:
  - 30 inches (76.2cm), square, 22-gauge, half-hard
  - 32 inches (81.3cm), half-round, 22-gauge, half-hard
- 14mm round faceted gem

tools and supplies

- water-soluble marker or pen
- fabric tape measure
- wire cutters
- polishing cloth
- chainnose pliers
- flatnose pliers
- roundnose pliers
- ring mandrel, marker, round dowel, or other small round object
- metal file

anatomy
of a
gemstone

This citrine is brilliant-cut, but many of the terms noted below are universally applicable to other lapidary cuts as well. Add these words to your jewelry-making vocabulary, and you'll impress your friends and family with your knowledge of a faceted gemstone's many faces.

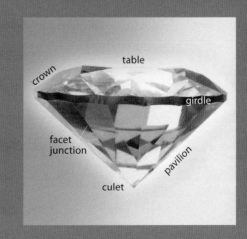

Chain Mail

Chain mail takes the beauty of wire and transforms it completely. Starting with a coil of wire, you can make many separate components, then reunite them, creating something completely new. The intricate patterns of chain mail jewelry are born from one simple technique, opening and closing jump rings, repeated in many different ways. Chain mail is experiencing a revival in popularity, and the wide selection of jump rings and wire available mean that it's easier than ever to get started. Unlike the solitary purpose of the little jump rings used to attach charms or clasps to bracelets and necklaces, the jump rings of chain mail work together en masse to create a textile, with a movement of links that makes it simply irresistible.

Chain concoction

Link a collection of jump rings in different sizes, shapes, and materials to create this delicate chain mail bracelet.

by Amy Robleski

C hain mail has a reputation for being hefty and masculine. If you were a medieval knight, you'd want your chain mail to be beefy and business-like – after all, the armor might be the only barrier between your tender flesh and an enemy's sword. Modern jewelry artists have discovered how to make chain mail that is far more delicate and decorative by joining jump rings in different sizes, gauges, and materials. The design possibilities are virtually limitless, ranging from stout chokers and formidable cuffs to the airy mixed-metal bracelet featured here.

Time constraints often make it impossible to finish a project in just one sitting, but this piece won't leave you short on satisfaction, even if you're forced to put it down. It's meant to be created in three easy stages. In fact, if you like the way the bracelet looks after the first or second stage, you can simply stop and wear it as-is.

Three-strand bracelet

Determine your bracelet's length. To get a base measurement, measure your wrist and subtract the length of your clasp. To estimate the number of copper jump rings you will need, multiply the base measurement by 9. A perfect fit is not essential for this bracelet because the clasp's extender makes it adjustable. For the number of oval sterling silver jump rings that your bracelet will require, multiply the base measurement by 11. For the number of round sterling silver jump rings, multiply the base measurement by 3.

These equations overestimate the quantities in case a jump ring becomes deformed or marred. The chain mail portion of the bracelet shown measures 5¾ inches (14.6cm): 48 copper jump rings, 60 oval jump rings, and 16 round jump rings were used.

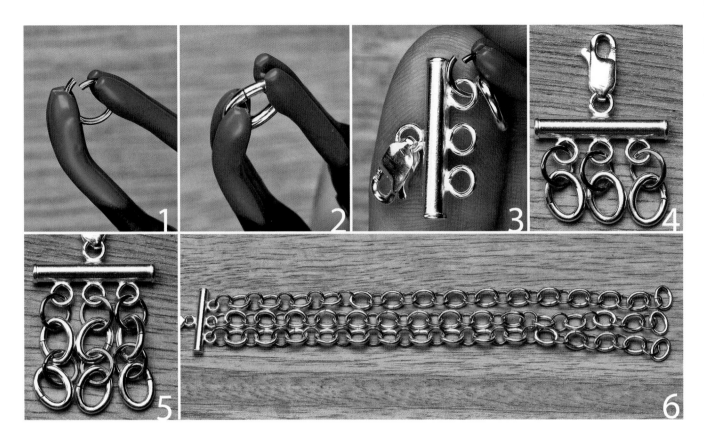

Open the copper jump rings. Open all the copper jump rings using two pairs of chainnose or bentnose pliers **[1]**. Do not open the jump rings more than halfway.

Securely close the oval jump rings. Set aside three oval jump rings for every inch of your bracelet's length; these will be used in the third stage. Securely close the rest of the oval jump rings by rotating the pliers back and forth until the ends of the jump rings are as aligned as possible **[2]**.

Attach jump rings to the clasp. Slide a closed oval jump ring onto an open copper jump ring. Attach the copper jump ring to a loop on the three-strand clasp **[3]**. Close the copper jump ring. Repeat this for the remaining clasp loops **[4]**.

Continue the chain pattern. Attach a copper jump ring to the last oval jump ring from the previous row and to a new oval jump ring. Close the copper jump ring. Repeat this step for all three rows **[5]**. Continue alternating copper and oval jump rings until you reach your desired length. It's best to work on all the rows continually rather than completing one row at a time. End the pattern with oval jump rings **[6]**.

Attach the remaining half of the clasp. Attach a copper jump ring to the last oval jump ring, then to the corresponding loop on the remaining half of the clasp **[7]**. Make sure your bracelet lies flat and straight when you do this; otherwise, the chains could become twisted. This is the first stopping point in the bracelet's construction.

Round jump rings

Open the round jump rings. Open all the round jump rings.

Attach the round jump rings. Using your dominant hand, carefully grasp one of the round jump rings with one pair of pliers. Holding the bracelet in your nondominant hand, align the first row of copper jump rings, and use the pliers to slide the round jump ring through all three copper jump rings **[8]**. Carefully close the jump ring. Working from the same side of the bracelet, continue to attach round jump rings to the rest of the copper rows until you have finished all the rows **[9]**. This is the second stopping point in the bracelet's construction.

Oval jump rings

Open the oval jump rings. Open all the remaining oval jump rings.

Attach the oval jump rings. Start on the same side of the bracelet as you did when you attached the round jump rings. As with the round jump rings, grasp one oval jump ring with one pair of pliers and slide it through the first row of oval jump rings **[10]**. Close the jump ring. Continue this pattern until you have finished all the rows **[11]**. Your bracelet is now complete.

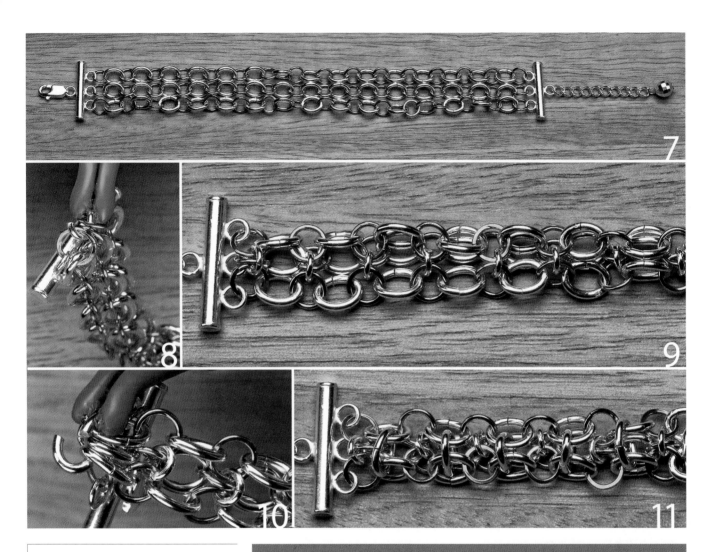

materials

- jump rings:
  - 50-81 copper, 20-gauge, 5mm inside diameter rounds
  - 61–99 sterling silver, 16-gauge, 5.3 x 3.2mm inside diameter ovals
  - 17–27 sterling silver, 18-gauge, 2.5mm inside diameter rounds
- three-strand clasp with extender chain, sterling-silver

tools and supplies

- 2 pairs of chainnose or bentnose pliers, or jump-ring-closing or nylon-jaw pliers (optional)
- Tool Magic rubber coating (optional)

avoid marring your jump rings

Beginners may notice that their pliers leave indentations and scratches on the sides of jump rings as they open and close them.

why does this happen?
The jaws of the pliers are made of metal that is harder than the metal of the jump rings. When you squeeze the pliers tightly, you push the jaws of the pliers into the jump rings, leaving marks.

how can I avoid this?
Keep your jump rings smooth by working with them gently. As you gain more experience opening and closing jump rings, you'll become comfortable exerting the right amount of pressure without marring the metal.

You can also purchase pliers with softer jaws, such as nylon-jaw pliers. Many jewelry artists cushion their pliers by wrapping the jaws with masking tape. In the photos shown, the pliers are covered with Tool Magic rubber coating.

Silken silver set

Link five types of jump rings for a sinfully slinky chain mail necklace and elegant, Persian-linked chain earrings with hand-forged earring frames.

by Julia Lowther

This Persian-linked chain mail necklace-and-earring set is a chameleon of fine jewelry. Conservative enough to drape over a demure turtleneck dress for a business dinner, it will also go beautifully with velvet to an opera or make a smashing focal point above a plunging neckline for a night on the town.

Although it may look complicated at first glance, the secret is simple. By using jump rings of graduated sizes, a static pattern takes on an exquisitely smooth, chic appearance after repetition. Chain mail connoisseurs will be left speechless by the flawless look and silken feel of this voluptuous piece.

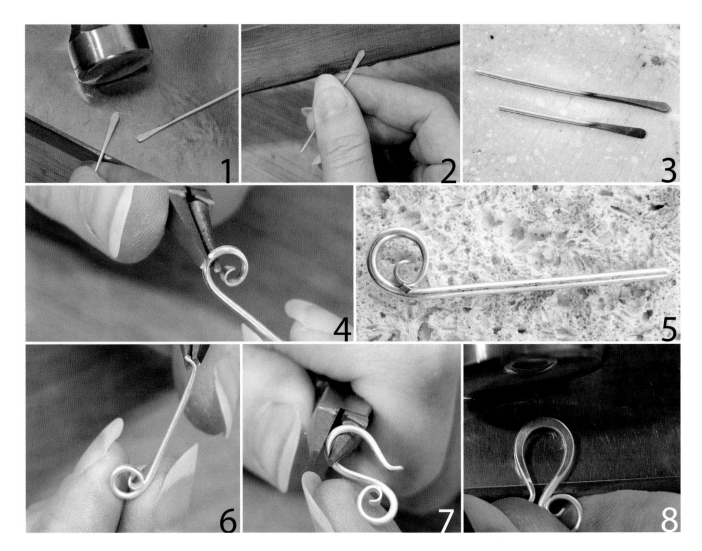

Necklace

Hook-and-eye clasp

Prepare the wires. Cut two pieces of 16-gauge sterling silver wire: one 1½ inches (38mm), the other 2 inches (51mm). Make sure each wire is straight. The short piece will become the eye, and the long piece will become the hook. Forge a flat paddle shape on one end of each wire using a planishing hammer and a bench block or anvil [1]. Burs may form on the tips of each paddle. Sand the burs smooth with 320- or 400-grit sandpaper [2]. Sand the short wire's unplanished end flat. Sand the long wire's unplanished end smooth and round.

Since you have work-hardened the wires by forging them, they must be annealed [3] before forming. Anneal the wires by heating them with a torch until the metal has a subtle pink color (dim or turn off the lights to help you see this color change). Remove the heat. Quench the pieces in water, place them in pickle to remove any dark-colored oxidation, and rinse.

Using combination pliers, roll the paddle of one wire into a curl, with the round jaw on the inside of the curl [4]. Roll until the flat section of the paddle touches the stem so that it can be soldered in place. Repeat with the other wire. If you use regular roundnose pliers, you will create small depressions on the outsides of the curls. You can space the depressions evenly around the outsides of the curls to convert a potential flaw into a pleasing design element. These "marks of process" are like fingerprints – they are unique to your piece and show that it was made by real working hands rather than by a machine.

Solder the hook. Flux only the long wire, and place it on a fire-resistant surface. Place a small pallion of easy solder where the curl touches the stem [5]. Heat the piece until the solder flows. Quench it in water, place it in warm pickle, and rinse it. Make sure the join is secure.

Shape the hook. Gently planish the rounded end of the long wire into a small paddle shape. Grasp this paddle with your combination pliers with the round jaw on the same side as the curl. Bend the paddle toward the curl at an 85-degree angle [6]. Grasp the stem halfway between the paddle and the curl with the flat jaw of your combination pliers on the same side of the wire as the curl. Gently shape the wire into a hook [7]. Planish the curved top of the hook [8].

Shape the eye. Make a loop on the straight end of the short wire. Adjust this loop to make the eye look like a figure 8 **[9]**.

Solder the eye. Flux the eye, and place it on a fire-resistant surface. Place small pallions of easy solder where the curl and the end of the simple loop touch the wire stem **[10]**. Heat the piece until the solder flows. Quench, pickle, and rinse it. Make sure the joins are secure.

Finish. Test the hook and the eye to make sure they are a good fit. Gently open or close the hook with your combination pliers to correct the fit, if necessary. Work-harden and restore the shine to your newly finished clasp by tumbling the pieces.

Tapered chain

Make the jump rings as specified in the materials list, or assemble premade jump rings.

Assemble the midsection of the chain. Begin by building the large midsection of the chain using 14-gauge jump rings.

Close two 14-gauge rings using chainnose and flatnose pliers or two pairs of parallel-jaw pliers. Link two 14-gauge rings through the two closed rings, and close this second pair. Link two 14-gauge rings through the last two rings added, and close this third pair **[11]**.

Attach a thin wire handle (24- to 26-gauge copper, or wire from a twist tie) to the four rings on one end **[12]**.

Hold the wire handle in your nondominant hand and your pliers in your dominant hand. Position the third pair of rings to the outsides of the first pair, creating a V **[13]**.

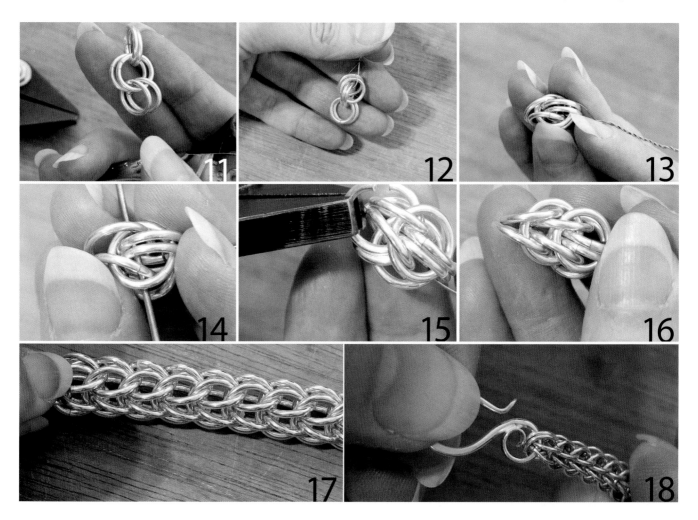

Cut a 3-inch (76mm) piece of thin wire to use as a guide, or use a needle for a sturdier guide. Slide your guide into the rings from the side: go between the second pair of rings, through the right third of the third pair of rings, and through the left third of the first pair of rings [14].

Follow the path of the guide with two open 14-gauge rings, one at a time. Close the rings away from the wire handle [15]. Attach two 14-gauge rings to the last pair added, and close them. Position the new rings outside of the previous V created [16]. Slide your guide in place through the new tier as before.

Repeat the pattern, placing your guide through the new tier each time, until all the 14-gauge rings are used [17].

Assemble the rest of the chain. For the rest of the jump rings, alternate between building one end of the chain and the other. Attach half of the rings of each size to one end and the other half to the other end. Gradually taper the necklace back to the clasp by assembling the rings in order of decreasing size. Repeating the pattern used for the midsection of the chain on each side, add:

> 28 16-gauge rings
> 32 18-gauge rings
> 44 20-gauge rings
> 60 22-gauge rings

Add or remove 22-gauge jump rings evenly on both ends of the necklace until you reach the proper length.

Attach the clasp. Gently open one of the last four rings on one end of the necklace. Slip the curl end of the hook through the ring, and close the ring. Repeat with the remaining three of the last four rings. When you are finished, the hook should be attached to the necklace by all four of the last rings on one end [18]. Repeat on the other end of the necklace to attach the eye half of the clasp.

Earrings

Earring frames

Prepare the wire. Cut two 1¼-inch (3.2cm) pieces of 16-gauge sterling silver wire. Make sure each wire is straight. Place the wire pieces on a bench block or anvil, and forge a flat paddle-shape on both ends using a planishing hammer [1]. Forge the paddle on one end of each wire a bit longer and wider than on the other [2]. Sand the burs on the tips of each paddle smooth with 320- or 400-grit sandpaper [3]. Since you have work-hardened the paddles by forging them, they must be annealed before they can be formed. Anneal them with a torch to a subtle pink color. Remove the heat. Quench the pieces in water, place them in pickle to remove any dark-colored oxidation, and rinse.

Form the curls. For the best results, the next several steps require combination pliers with one round jaw and one flat jaw. However, regular roundnose pliers will also do the job.

Hold one piece of wire by the tip of the smaller paddle, and roll up the paddle with the round jaw on the inside [4]. Roll until the tip of the paddle touches the metal it is rolled up against, as the rolled paddle will be soldered into a ring. The chain will dangle from this small ring.

Roll the large paddle into a large, loose curl in the opposite direction of the small paddle [5]. Roll until the flat part of the large paddle touches the wire near the rolled-up small paddle so that it can be soldered in place.

Repeat for the second earring frame, making it the mirror image of the first [6].

Solder the frames. Use the point of a soldering pick to crush two small depressions into a firebrick that will allow your earring frames to lie flat. Flux one frame, and place it in a depression. Place two small pallions of medium solder on the frame – one where the small paddle touches the central piece of wire and one where the large paddle touches the wire. Flux the second frame, and put the medium-solder pallions in place [7]. Heat both frames until the solder flows. Quench, pickle, rinse, and check that the joins are secure.

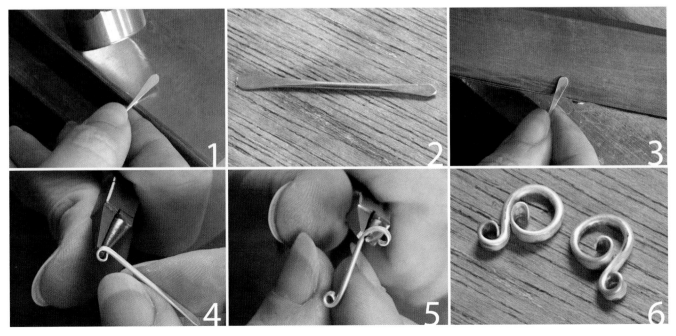

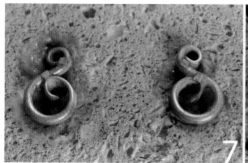  

Solder ear posts. Flux one frame again, and place it in a firebrick depression. Grasp a sterling silver ear post in a pair of cross-lock tweezers, and flux it. (If you are not using a purchased post, use a 3/8-inch/9.5mm piece of 20-gauge wire.) Position the post vertically, with its end pressed firmly against the central part of the earring frame between the small paddle and the large one **[8]**. Place a pallion of easy solder at the base of the post. Carefully heat the earrings and the posts until the solder flows. Allow the piece to cool to ensure that the join is secure. Quench, pickle, and rinse.

Grasp the post in a pair of flatnose pliers, and twist it one-quarter of a turn. This will harden the post, since it has been annealed by soldering. It will also test the join to make sure it is sound. The post can be hardened further by horizontally grasping it close to the frame with chainnose pliers and grasping it lengthwise with flatnose pliers. Twist the flatnose pliers to work-harden the post **[9]**.

Solder a post to the second earring frame and harden it the same way.

Polish. Tumble your earring frames and posts with ceramic medium, or brush them with a brass brush and soap and water for a more subtle finish.

Chain drops

Assemble the chain. Work from the bottom of the earring to the top. Close two 16-gauge rings. Link two open 16-gauge rings through the two closed rings, and close the second set of rings **[10]**. Link two large 18-gauge rings through the last two 16-gauge rings, and close them **[11]**.

materials

necklace

- sterling silver jump rings and round, half-hard wire:
  - 40 14-gauge, 8.7mm inside diameter (ID) jump rings or 5 feet (1.5m) 14-gauge wire and an 11/32-inch (8.7mm) mandrel
  - 56 16-gauge, 6.7mm ID jump rings or 7½ feet (2.3m) 16-gauge wire and a 17/64-inch (6.7mm) mandrel
  - 64 18-gauge, 5.5mm ID jump rings or 12 feet (3.6m) 18-gauge wire and a 7/32-inch (5.5mm) mandrel
  - 88 20-gauge, 4.4mm ID jump rings or 19 feet (5.8m) 20-gauge wire and an 11/64-inch (4.4mm) mandrel
  - 120 22-gauge, 3.6mm ID jump rings or 31 feet (9.4m) 22-gauge wire and a 9/64-inch (3.6mm) mandrel
  - 4 inches (10.2cm) 16-gauge wire for the clasp

(Note: If you are buying premade jump rings and cannot find the exact inside diameter needed, choose the closest diameter that is larger than the diameter called for. The author used a punch set indexed from 3/32 inch to 1/64 inch as dowels for her jump rings.)

earrings

- sterling silver jump rings or round, half-hard wire:
  - 8 16-gauge, 6.7mm inside diameter (ID) jump rings or 14 inches (35.6cm) 16-gauge wire and a 17/64-inch (6.7mm) mandrel
  - 8 18-gauge, 5.5mm ID jump rings or 12 inches (30.5cm) 18-gauge wire and a 7/32-inch (5.5mm) mandrel
  - 2 18-gauge, 3.6mm ID jump rings or 2 inches (5.1cm) 18-gauge wire and a 9/64-inch (3.6) mandrel
  - 8 20-gauge, 4.4mm ID jump rings or 6 inches (15.2cm) 20-gauge wire and an 11/64-inch (4.4mm) mandrel
  - 8 22-gauge, 3.6mm ID jump rings or 6 inches (15.2cm) 22-gauge wire and a 9/64-inch (3.6mm) mandrel
- 2 sterling silver ear posts, or 2 3/8-inch (9.5mm) pieces of 20-gauge wire
- 2 sterling silver ear nuts

tools and supplies

- wire cutters
- steel bench block or anvil
- planishing hammer
- sanding stick, 320 or 400 grit
- soldering station: torch, easy solder, fire-resistant surface (soldering pad, firebrick, or charcoal block), pickle pot with pickle, flux, steel tweezers (cross locking and precision), and copper tongs
- combination (one round jaw and one flat jaw) or roundnose pliers
- chainnose and flatnose, or two pairs parallel jaw
- tumbler with ceramic tumbling media and burnishing liquid
- scrap silver (optional)
- liver of sulfur (optional)
- transfer punch set or mandrels of appropriate diameters (optional)
- hand drill, cordless drill, or winder (optional)
- jeweler's saw, 2/0 blades (optional)
- needle or 6 inches (15.2cm) 24- to 26-gauge copper or scrap wire

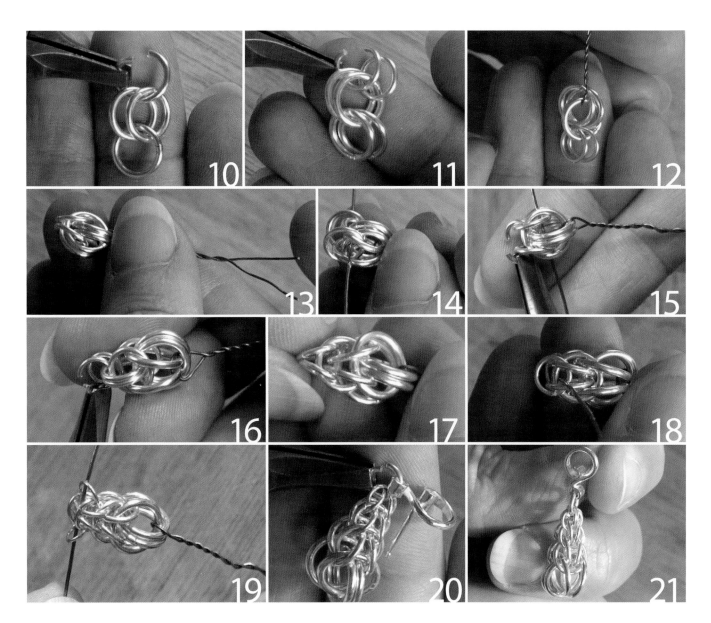

Attach a thin wire handle (24- to 26-gauge copper, or the wire from a twist tie) to hold the four 16-gauge rings **[12]**.

Hold the wire handle in your non-dominant hand and your pliers in your dominant hand. Position the two large 18-gauge rings to the outsides of the first two 16-gauge rings **[13]**.

Cut a piece of thin wire, about 3 inches (76mm) long, to use as a guide. You can use a needle if you prefer a sturdier guide. Slide your guide into the rings from the side: go between the second set of 16-gauge rings, through the right third of the large 18-gauge rings, and through the left third of the first set of 16-gauge rings **[14]**.

Follow the path of the guide with two open, large 18-gauge rings, one at a time **[15]**. Close the rings with their openings facing to the left.

Attach two 20-gauge rings to the last two large 18-gauge rings that were added. Close them **[16]**. Position the 20-gauge rings just added to the outsides of the V of the large 18-gauge rings **[17]**. Slide your guide in place as in step 8, just on a separate tier **[18]**.

Follow the path of the guide with two open 20-gauge rings, one at a time. Close the rings.

Attach two 22-gauge rings to the two 20-gauge rings that were just added. Position the 22-gauge rings just added to the outsides of the V of 20-gauge rings, and place your guide wire as before **[19]**.

Follow the path of the guide with two open 22-gauge rings, one at a time. Close the rings.

Lastly, link one small 18-gauge ring through all four 22-gauge rings and

through the small curl of one earring frame **[20]**. Close that ring and you have finished one earring **[21]**.

Make the second earring. Assemble the second earring following the same pattern and go out in style, bedecked in your new Persian glory!

Cold Connections

Cold connections allow jewelry makers to join different jewelry components, beads, metal shapes, and more, into gorgeous finished jewelry pieces. The name comes from the fact that all the pieces in the jewelry are combined without the use of heat – no torches or kilns are used to join or set the elements. This makes cold connections a great starting point for beginners, who may not have a wide selection of advanced tools. It also allows a unique opportunity for creativity. The joining of the components – the coils, hinges, and loops – are as much a focal point as the components themselves. The art of cold connections comes from the way the entire piece fits together with the beauty of a mobile, three-dimensional sculpture.

Strike
it rich

Hit the mother lode with this matching bracelet-and-earring set composed of sterling silver coins, carnelian gemstones, and silver coils.

by Gretta Van Someren

L ight reflects off the silver coins and coils sported by this fashionable duo. Carnelian gemstone beads are tucked away in the wire coils, bringing a hint of color to the bracelet and earrings. Casual yet classy, you'll enjoy the jingle-jangle of this set wherever you go.

The techniques below show how to make a bracelet 8¼ inches (21cm) long. (To tailor the fit to your wrist, adjust the length of the wrapped-loop connectors or the number or size of the jump rings you use.) Use the same techniques to create coordinating earrings.

Bracelet

Prepare the coins. Take two 1-inch (2.5cm) and one ¾-inch (19mm) sterling-silver coins and pierce two holes in each coin; position the holes at opposite ends. (These holes allow you to connect the pieces.) To pierce, place the coin on a steel bench block. Rest the tip of a center punch ⅛ inch (3mm) from the edge of the coin and tap with the flat end of a chasing hammer **[1]** to dimple the metal, which will guide the drill bit. Remove the metal from the bench block. Drill holes using an electric drill with a #46 bit and file smooth.

Stamp the coins. Place a coin on the steel bench block, holding the stamping tool in place with your recessive hand. With your dominant hand, firmly tap the tool with the flat edge of a chasing hammer until an impression is made **[2]**.

Mold the shape. Carefully create slight curves in the coins using a dapping block and punch and a rawhide or plastic mallet **[3]**. Tap lightly or you'll mar the stamped images.

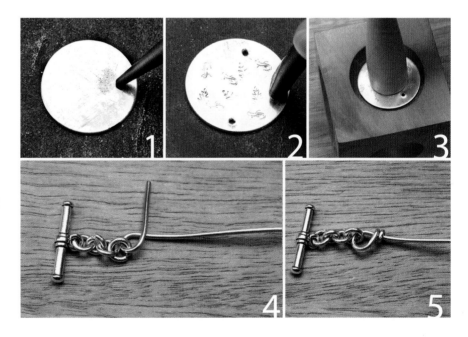

Connect the first piece. Connect four jump rings to one end of a toggle clasp. Loop a 4-inch (10.2cm) piece of 16-gauge, dead-soft, round wire onto the bottom jump ring **[4]**, and wrap that end of the wire twice around the stem of the wire, making a wrapped loop **[5]**. Bend the wire up at a 90-degree angle and string

the ¾-inch (19mm) coin and a spacer bead, and use roundnose and flatnose pliers to create a coil at the top of the coin. Press the coil snugly against the spacer bead to make sure it is secure **[6]**.

Add the wire-wrapped bead. Use an 8-inch (20.3cm) piece of 22-gauge, half-

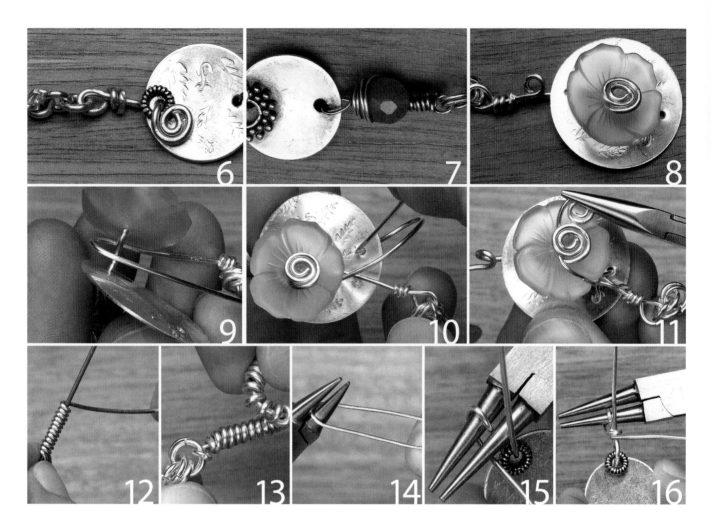

hard wire to loop through the other hole in the ¾-inch (19mm) coin. Wrap the wire around the stem a few times and slide an 8mm bead onto the other end of the wire. Using the same wire that you used to make the wraps around the stem, make several wraps around the top third of the bead to crown it. With the stem wire, make the first half of a wrapped loop, attach two soldered jump rings, and finish the wraps. Bring the tail of the wire that crowned the bead around the bead and down to the bottom and wrap it around the stem several times. Cut any excess wire and tuck in the ends [7].

Secure the centerpiece bead. Using a 9-inch (22.9cm) piece of 16-gauge wire, start a wrapped loop and connect it to the two jump rings in the previous step. Finish the wraps. (In this example, a loop was added after the wraps for aesthetics and to take up excess wire.) Bring the wire up through a hole in the coin and through the centerpiece bead. To secure the bead in place, create a

large coil on top of the bead and press it down against the bead [8].

Using an 8-inch (20.3cm) piece of 16-gauge wire, begin a wrapped loop, attach three jump rings, and complete the wraps. Trim the tail and tuck it under. Take the other end of the wire and loop it around the wire on the underside of the centerpiece bead (think of lassoing the wire) [9]. (It will be a tight squeeze to fit the wire under the bead – we extended the space beneath the bead to illustrate.) Bring it back around toward the open hole in the coin, crossing the wire over itself, and come up through the hole from the bottom side [10]. Create a spiral with this wire on top of the centerpiece bead, but underneath the existing coil. Connect two jump rings to the three jump rings on the wrapped loop [11].

Make a coiled connector. Wrap 10–18 inches (25.4–45.7cm) of 16-gauge wire around a thin mandrel; a piece of 14-gauge steel rod was used in this example [12]. Cut a 4-inch (10.2cm) piece

of 18-gauge wire. Make a small loop on one end of the wire, and connect the loop to the two jump rings on the end of the bracelet. Thread the 16-gauge coil onto the wire and make another loop. Shape the coiled connector to your liking [13].

Add the last coin. Open a jump ring attach the loop at the end of the bracelet to one side of the last 1-inch (2.5cm) coin.

Bend a 4-inch (10.2cm) piece of 16-gauge wire in half [14]. Center the other hole in the coin and an 8mm flat spacer bead in the bend. With one wire, start a wrapped loop approximately ⅜ inch (9.5mm) from the top of the coin [15]. Finish the loop by wrapping the tail around both wires, binding the two together [16]. Trim the tail.

Attach a jump ring to the wrapped loop. Attach a jump ring to this jump ring, and use a third jump ring to attach the clasp to the second jump ring. Bend the remaining wire at a 90-degree angle and press it down against the wrapped wires. Trim the wire short with wire cutters or form the wire into a coil.

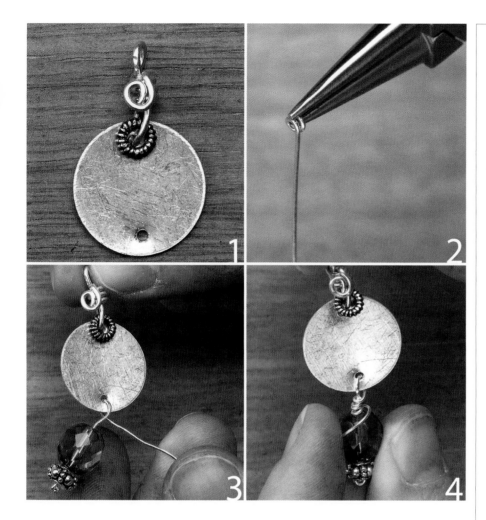

materials

bracelet

- 2 1-inch (2.5cm), 22-gauge, sterling silver coins
- ¾-inch (19mm), 22-gauge, sterling silver coin
- 16-gauge, dead-soft, sterling silver, round wire
- assorted jump rings
- silver toggle clasp
- 2 8–10mm flat silver spacer beads
- 18-gauge, half-hard, sterling silver, round wire
- 8mm round bead
- large bead

earrings

- 2 ¾-inch (19mm), 22-gauge, sterling silver coins
- 18-gauge, half-hard, sterling silver, round wire
- 2 8mm flat spacer beads
- 22-gauge, dead-soft, sterling silver, round wire
- 2 4mm silver beads
- 2 8mm round beads
- pair of French ear wires

tools and supplies

- steel bench block
- ruler
- center punch
- chasing hammer
- drill (with #46 bit)
- needle files
- flatnose pliers
- roundnose pliers
- wire cutters
- stamping tool
- dapping block
- rawhide or plastic mallet
- thin mandrel
- liver of sulfur (optional)
- tumbler with stainless steel shot and burnishing compound (optional)

Finishing touches. Check all wire ends for any rough edges and file if necessary. Patinate with liver of sulfur or another oxidizing agent to bring out the stamped images. Be careful not to get liver of sulfur on any porous or delicate gemstones. For a satin or shiny finish, place in a tumbler with stainless steel shot and burnishing compound and tumble for 15–30 minutes.

Earrings

When making wire earrings, perform each step of the design to both earrings before moving on to the next step. This will ensure more symmetrical pieces.

Prepare the coins. Drill holes in two ¾-inch (19mm) coins and file the holes as you did for the bracelet. Stamp or texture the coins (or leave them blank) and give them a slightly convex shape using a dapping block.

Create the wrap. Bend a 4-inch (10.2cm) piece of 16-gauge wire in half and string a coin and a spacer. With the wires extending upward, make the first half of a wrapped loop with the back wire ⅜ inch (9.5mm) from the top of the coin. Finish the loop by wrapping the tail around both wires, binding them together. Bend the other wire at a 90-degree angle, press it down against the wraps, and coil the end **[1]**.

Create the dangle. Cut two 4-inch (10.2cm) pieces of 22-gauge wire. Make a very small coil at the end of each piece of wire **[2]** and string a 4mm silver bead followed by an 8mm bead. Make the first half of a wrapped loop above the 8mm bead, and attach the other hole of the coin **[3]**. Finish the loop by wrapping the tail around the stem and the top of the bead, making a cap. Wrap the wire down and around the bead, making a few wraps at the base to secure the end **[4]**. Trim the tail.

Finishing touches. Attach ear wires. If necessary, adjust the direction of your wire loop using flatnose pliers. Patinate and polish as you did for the bracelet, if desired.

Geometry lesson

Add texture and dimension to simple metal shapes and link them together for a sophisticated bracelet.

by Wendy Witchner

The simplest of geometrics – ovals, rectangles, and triangles – have inspired artists for centuries. Let the symmetrical beauty of this oval bracelet inspire you to mix your own formula of metal and wire. You may begin with precut metal components and concentrate on refining your wireworking skills, or you can cut your own unusual shapes, add interesting textures, and make free-form connectors.

Create the metal shapes. If you're using purchased oval metal components, skip this step. Otherwise, place a piece of Glad® Press 'n Seal™ plastic on top of the oval pattern, p. 88. Use a fine-tip permanent marker to trace the oval five times onto the plastic; mark the positions of the dots, too. (*Editor's Note:* The oval bracelet shown on p. 84 is 7¼ inches/18.4cm long. Either add another oval or adjust the spiral connectors for a longer bracelet.) Peel up the plastic and press it onto 22-gauge sheet metal. Using tin snips, or a jeweler's saw with a 4/0 or 5/0 blade and a bench pin, cut out your shapes. Use a nail or center punch to make a small indentation at each dot. Remove the plastic from the metal.

Texture the metal shapes. To make the surface of the metal shapes more interesting, place a texturing sheet on top of the shapes, then hammer them, or use an engraved hammer and pound the shapes without the texture sheet **[1]**. File the edges smooth **[2]**.

Drill the holes in the metal shapes. The indentations at the dots mark where the holes should go. The center and end holes should snugly accommodate the twisted wire; use a #54 (.055-inch) bit for these holes **[3]**. The side holes will accommodate jump rings, which should fit loosely to allow for movement, so use a #52 (.063-inch) bit for these holes **[4]**.

Coil the twisted wire. Cut a 6-inch (15.2cm) piece of twisted wire. Using chainnose pliers, make a right-angle bend ¼ inch (6.5mm) from one end. Insert the bent end into the center hole. Following the lines of the metal shape, use your fingers to spiral the twisted wire **[5]**. When you've reached the other twisted-wire hole, bend the wire at a right angle and slide it through the hole **[6]**. Trim the tail to ¼ inch.

Form the connector spirals. Cut a 2½-inch (6.4cm) piece of 16-gauge wire. Use roundnose pliers to form the wire into a spiral **[7]**. Cut off any excess and file the end. Add texture and harden the wire by lightly hammering the spiral **[8]**. Bend the outer end of the spiral flush with the spiral to close it. Make a total of five small spirals.

Curve the shapes. Remove the spiral from a metal shape, place the metal shape, face down, in the largest hole of a dapping block and use the dapping punch to press on the metal shape **[9]**. This will cause the shape to gently cup, creating an attractive convex profile. Repeat with the other shapes.

Add patina. If desired, use liver of sulfur or a blackening agent to add depth to the metal pieces, the twisted-wire spirals, the smaller connector spirals, and the jump rings. Polish to remove the patina on the top layers, so it shows only in the crevices.

multishape
bracelet

Make the 7¼-inch (18.4cm) multishape bracelet following the instructions for the oval bracelet, with the exceptions noted below.

Create the metal shapes.
Trace one rectangle, one triangle, and two ovals on the Press 'n Seal™. File the edges, rounding the points.

Drill the holes.
The center holes and the holes placed off-center at one end of the oval pieces need to fit snugly around the twisted wire. The remaining holes at the ends of each piece will also accommodate twisted wire, but these holes should be larger, to allow for some movement.

Form the twisted wire.
On the more angular pieces, you may need to use chainnose or flat-nose pliers to form the corners of the spiral. After you slide the twisted wire into an end hole of the triangle and rectangle, trim the twisted wire ½ inch (13mm) from the edge of the metal shape. For the ovals, slide the twisted wire into the off-center hole. Do not trim the excess at this time.

Form the connector spirals.
The connector spirals are made from twisted wire with a loop at one end to replace the jump ring. Cut a 4-inch (10.2cm) piece of 20-gauge twisted wire. Start at one end and form a three-round spiral. After the third round, bend the wire at a right angle away from the spiral. Trim the wire, leaving a ½-inch tail. Form the tail into a plain loop, perpendicular to the spiral. Make a total of three spirals.

Join the spirals and shapes.
Bend the tail in the center hole back and tap it lightly with a hammer. For the triangle and rectangle, bend the ½-inch tail at one end away from the shape. Form the tail into a plain loop, perpendicular to the shape, to link to the connector spiral. For the ovals, bring the remaining wire from the wrong side through the off-center hole to the right side in the nearby centered hole at the end. Trim the wire to ½ inch and make a plain loop; keep the cut end toward the wrong side of the shape and the loop perpendicular to the shape.

Join the pieces to form the bracelet.
Open the loop at one end of an oval shape, slide the hook clasp on the loop, and close the loop. Open the loop on a connector spiral, slide the open hole at the other end of this oval shape on the loop, and close the loop. Open the loop on the rectangle shape, link it through the outer round of the previously joined spiral, and close the loop. Repeat in this manner, adding the triangle and the oval. Insert a jump ring through the remaining hole in the oval, linking additional jump rings if needed for length.

patterns for multishape bracelet

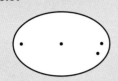

oval

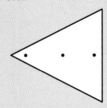

triangle

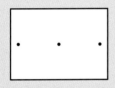

rectangle

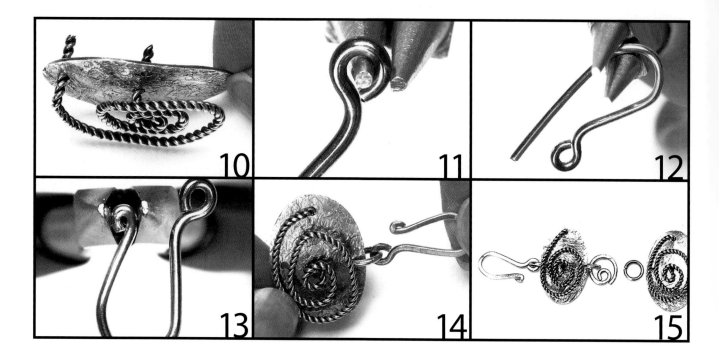

Join the spirals and shapes. Insert the spirals into the holes drilled in their corresponding shapes **[10]**. Bend the tails over on the back of the metal shape and trim the tails short, bending and flattening them with a tap of a hammer to keep them in place.

Make the clasp. Cut a 2½-inch (6.4cm) piece of 16- or 18-gauge wire. Turn a loop on one end **[11]**. Using roundnose pliers, form the wire into a hook **[12]**. Trim any excess wire and turn back the tip of the wire to form a tiny loop **[13]**. Hammer the entire clasp on a bench block to strengthen it.

Join the pieces to form a bracelet. Open a jump ring, slide it into a side hole of one metal shape and the loop of the hook clasp **[14]**. Close the jump ring. Open another jump ring and slide it through the other side hole. Link it through one of the connector spirals and close the jump ring. Join the other side of the connector spiral to another metal shape using a jump ring **[15]**. Continue until the bracelet is the desired length, ending with two jump rings or a spiral shape.

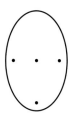

pattern for oval bracelet

materials
oval bracelet
- 5 22x29mm 22-gauge sterling silver ovals or 1 x 6-inch (2.5x5.2cm) 22-gauge sterling silver sheet
- 36 inches (91.4cm) .056-inch-diameter twisted wire made by twisting two 20-gauge wires
- 18 inches (45.7cm) 16-gauge wire
- 1 or more 6mm 16-gauge jump rings
- 2½ inches (6.4cm) 16- or 18-gauge wire

multishape bracelet
- 1x6-inch (2.5x5.2cm) 22-gauge sterling silver sheet
- 3½ feet (1.1m) .056-inch-diameter twisted wire made by twisting two 20-gauge wires
- 1 or more 6mm 16-gauge jump rings
- 2½ inches (6.4cm) 16- or 18-gauge wire

tools and supplies
- fine-tip marker
- Glad® Press 'n Seal™ plastic wrap
- nail or center punch to mark holes
- tin snips or jeweler's saw with 4/0 or 5/0 blade and bench pin
- texturing sheet and plain hammer or engraved hammer
- bench block or anvil
- metal files
- drill or pin vise with #54 and #52 (.055- and .063-inch) bit
- wire cutters
- chainnose pliers
- roundnose pliers
- dapping block with punch
- liver of sulfur (optional)
- polishing cloth

Santa Fe
dreaming

Give a new twist to Native American-inspired, stamped metal.

by Connie Fox

M etalwork and wire wrapping combine to create a bracelet that evokes the signature silverwork of New Mexican artists. The faceplate allows for a variety of stamped designs, and the layers of wrapped wire give the bracelet serious heft. Let the switchback curves of the wire clasp conjure up the mountains of the American Southwest.

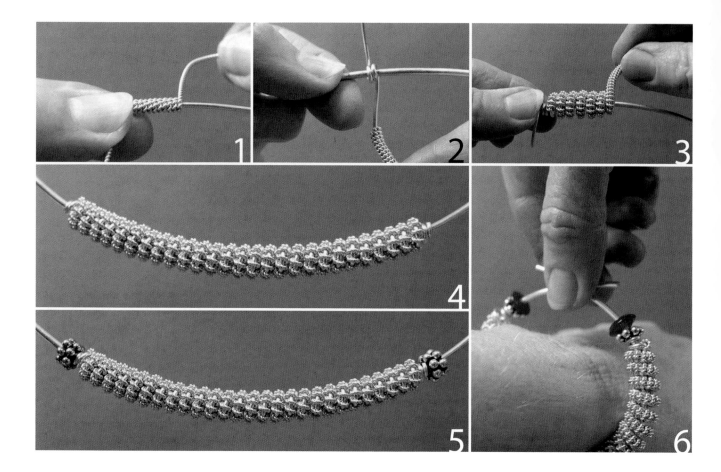

Measure and cut the wire. Measure your wrist and add 2¾ inches (70mm). Cut a piece of 12-gauge sterling silver round wire to this length. This will become the armature for the bracelet. Cut 30 inches (76.2cm) of 16-gauge wire to serve as the base wire. Cut 10 feet (3m) of 22-gauge twisted wire.

Wrap the twisted wire around the base wire. Measure to the midpoint of the twisted wire, and center it on the base wire. Wrap one half of the twisted wire clockwise around the base wire [1]. Turn the wire over and wrap the other half around the base wire. Trim the unwrapped ends of the twisted wire flush. The twisted, wrapped wire will be able to slide along the base wire.

Wrap around the armature wire. Wrap one end of the base wire around the armature wire twice [2]. Slide the twisted, wrapped wire up to the armature wire. Coil the twisted, wrapped wire around the armature wire [3]. Wrap the excess base wire around the armature wire twice. Cut off any excess base wire [4].

Add spacers for a custom-fit bracelet. To achieve a good fit, use spacers to increase the size of the bracelet body. The number of spacers required will vary [5].

Curve the armature to form a bracelet. Curve the bracelet armature over a bracelet mandrel to create a cuff shape. Slide one spacer on each end of the armature wire. Grasp the two ends of the armature wire, and curve the wire around your wrist [6]. Leave 2 inches (51mm) on each end for the end loops and

get twisted

When purchasing twisted wire, check with the supplier to ensure that you are receiving two pieces of wire that have been twisted together. Some sources sell "twisted" wire that is actually an extruded variation. This latter type of wire is not truly twisted, and will not yield the same results.

Make your own twisted wire by bending 22-gauge round wire in half lengthwise and clamping the ends in a bench vice. Use a hook installed into your flex shaft to hold the bend. Pull the wire taut, and gently apply speed with the foot pedal. Work slowly, as the spinning hook will quickly twist your wire.

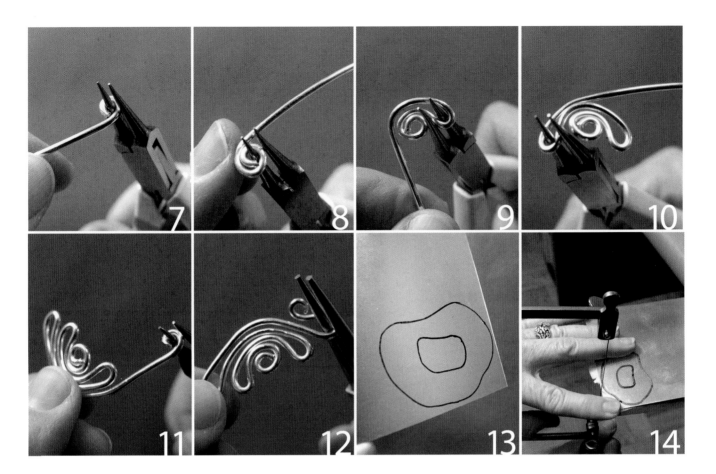

the clasp. Add spacers to determine the ideal fit, and trim the excess armature wire. A snug, but not tight, fit will prevent the faceplate of the bracelet from turning.

Make the loops to fasten the clasp. Make a loop at one end of the armature wire, rolling the loop toward the center of the bracelet. Make an identically sized loop on the other end of the bracelet, and trim any excess armature wire.

Make the switchback clasp. Cut a 7-inch (17.8cm) piece of 14-gauge sterling silver round wire. File the end smooth. Use small roundnose pliers to make a loop at one end [7]. Continue to coil the wire one half revolution around the small loop [8]. Holding the wire close to the coil, bend the wire back around the roundnose pliers to create the first outer curve of the clasp [9]. Repeat on the other side of the coil to make the second outer curve [10]. Bend the wire in the reverse direction one more time to create the switchback outer curve. Measure 1 inch (2.5cm) beyond the last outer curve, and cut the wire. File the end. Use roundnose pliers to make a small loop

at the end of the wire [11]. Make a curve in the opposite direction from the loop to form a hook [12]. Hammer the four outside curves of the clasp to work-harden the clasp. This will slightly open the curves; use chainnose pliers to bend them tight again. Open one loop at the end of the bracelet body to attach the clasp.

Make the faceplate. Draw a template for the faceplate on cardstock. Cut out the template, and use a permanent marker to transfer the faceplate shape to 22-gauge sterling silver sheet [13]. Saw along the outside perimeter of the faceplate, using a smooth motion and holding the metal in the open V section of the bench pin [14]. Use a center punch, bench block, and

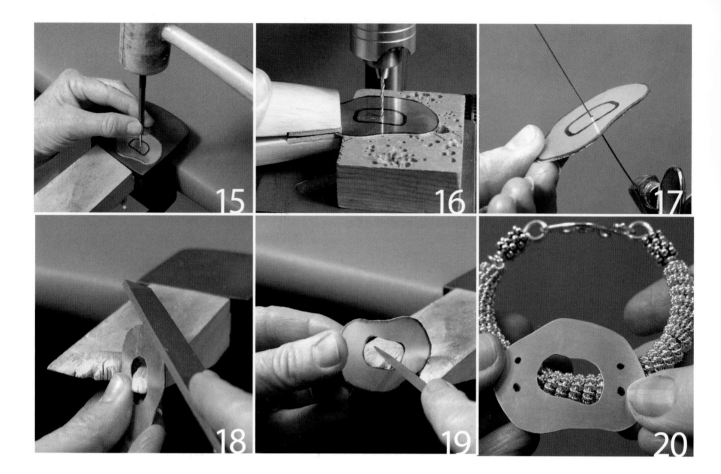

mallet to create a dimple in the center section of the faceplate [15]. Place the faceplate on a piece of wood. Secure the faceplate with a ring clamp, and drill a hole through the dimple [16].

Remove one end of the saw blade from the saw frame. Slide the blade through the hole in the faceplate, then reinsert the blade into the saw frame, and tighten [17]. Saw out the inside section of the faceplate. Remove one end of the blade from the saw frame to remove the faceplate.

Wedge the faceplate into the V section of the bench pin. Use a flat hand file with a straight, forward motion to file the outer edge smooth [18]. Use a half-round needle or hand file to file the inside curve of the faceplate [19]. Use sandpaper to smooth the filed edges.

Mark and drill the attachment holes.
Position the faceplate on top of the bracelet to determine where to drill the attachment holes. Mark one pair of attachment holes on each side of the center hole [20]. The holes should be far enough from the edge of the faceplate to prevent the metal from tearing due to

stress. Drill the attachment holes in the faceplate, and file any burs off the back.

Stamp and shape the faceplate. Draw a design in pencil on the cardstock template. Transfer the design to the faceplate with a permanent marker [21]. Tape the faceplate to an anvil. Stamp the faceplate using design stamps, a center punch, or other hardened steel tools and a chasing hammer [22]. Place the faceplate on a bracelet mandrel or rolling pin. Tap the faceplate with a rawhide mallet to shape it into a curve.

Polish and patinate. Polish the faceplate and bracelet with a polishing cloth, or use a polishing machine with polishing compound on a buff. If desired, patinate the bracelet and faceplate with liver of sulfur according to the manufacturer's instructions. Rinse, dry, and then clean the components with a brass brush and soapy water.

Attach the faceplate. Cut a 6-inch (15.2cm) piece of 18-gauge round wire. Using roundnose pliers, make a U in the

middle of the wire. Center the faceplate on top of the bracelet. From back to front, thread the ends of the U through one pair of holes in the faceplate [23]. Keeping the curve of the U secure against the back of the bracelet, bend each protruding end across the adjacent hole without crossing the wires [24]. Slide one wire end through the adjacent hole to the back of the faceplate [25]. Repeat with the other wire end. Pull the wires to tighten them against the bracelet.

Keeping the faceplate snug against the bracelet, cross the wire ends [26]. Cut the wire ends so that each is 1 inch (2.5cm) long. Coil each wire end, and tuck it against the bracelet [27].

Attach the other side of the faceplate to the bracelet the same way.

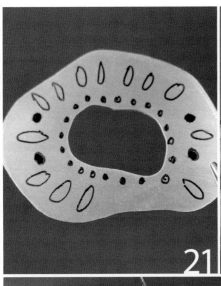

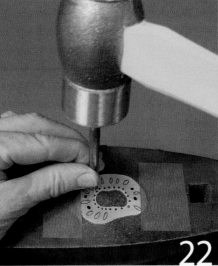

materials

- sterling silver wire:
  - 3 yards (2.7m) 22-gauge twisted, dead-soft
  - 12 inches (30.5cm) 18-gauge round, dead-soft
  - 30 inches (76.2cm) 16-gauge round, dead-soft
  - 7 inches (17.8cm) 14-gauge round, dead-soft
  - 11 inches (27.9cm) 12-gauge round, dead-soft
  - 20 feet (6m) 22-gauge round, dead-soft (optional)
- 11 inches (27.9cm) 12-gauge copper wire, round, dead-soft (optional)
- 4–14 sterling silver spacers to fit 12-gauge (2.1mm) wire
- 22-gauge (0.6mm) sterling silver or copper sheet, dead-soft, 2½ x 2 inches (64 x 51mm)
- beads (optional)

tools and supplies

- wire cutters
- bracelet mandrel or rolling pin
- chainnose pliers
- flatnose pliers
- long roundnose pliers
- small roundnose pliers
- hand files
- needle files
- rawhide mallet
- bench block or anvil
- cardstock
- permanent marker
- jeweler's saw, 2/0 or 3/0 blade
- bench pin
- center punch
- safety glasses
- particulate mask
- ring clamp
- drill press or flex shaft, 1mm twist drill bit
- sandpaper: various grits
- design stamps (optional)
- finishing items: polishing cloth or polishing machine with polishing compound and buff
- liver of sulfur (optional)
- brass brush (optional)
- lubricant (beeswax)
- magnifiers (optional)
- painters' tape

modify the design

- Substitute copper sheet metal for the sterling silver sheet metal.
- Add beads in Santa Fe colors.
- Rivet a piece of sheet metal to the faceplate to add dimension.

Soldered Connections

Why include soldering in a wire book? It's true that many wire artists focus exclusively on creating beautiful wire pieces without a torch. However, adding heat to the process can significantly alter the capabilities of wire, adding an entirely new element to jewelry design. The delicate yet secure chains and seamless chandelier shapes featured in this chapter could not be accomplished without soldering, yet the focus of these jewelry pieces is on the flexibility and beauty of wire as a medium. If you're new to soldering, be sure to check out our Basics section. You also will find plenty of resources (in books and on the Internet) if you find you need a little more encouragement and instruction to get started. Begin by learning about the different tools and materials involved and what they do, and then get ready to experience the magic of adding heat to your jewelry making. Don't be afraid to try something new!

Link to the past

From the far distant past comes this ancient chain-link technique that's simple to solder and even easier to assemble.

by Leslee Frumin

Simple and versatile, this soldered chain-link technique adds a classic touch to any jewelry wardrobe. For an unadorned bracelet or necklace, the folded links make a sensuous and slinky chain. If you are looking for a foundation to show off your favorite beads and charms, the large links provide the perfect base to highlight your collection.

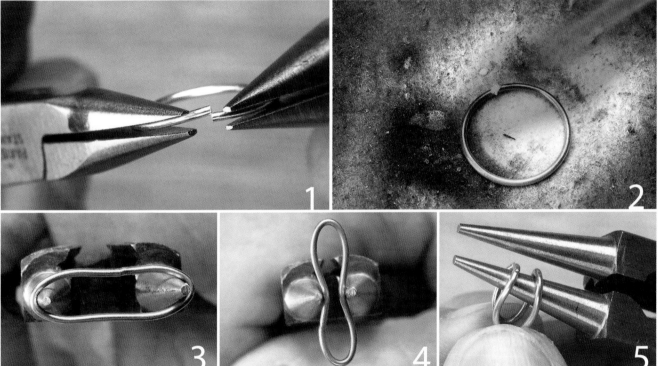

Make the jump rings. Use 20-gauge, dead-soft, sterling silver wire to make the jump rings. Ten feet of wire yields approximately 50 ½-inch (13mm) inner-diameter rings, which is more than enough for a 7- to 8-inch (17.8–20.3cm) bracelet. Fifty rings may sound like too many, but you'll want to make more than you think you'll need because it's easy to damage a ring as you make the links. Use a ½-inch (13mm) diameter mandrel to make the jump rings.

Close each jump ring fully to prepare them for soldering **[1]**. Prepare pallions of solder to solder the jump rings closed. Use one piece of solder for each jump ring.

Place a closed ring on the firing brick and paint a small amount of paste flux over the join. Put a fine tip on the torch and heat the flux until it glazes over. Use a solder pick or tweezers to place a piece of solder on the join **[2]**. Keep the torch moving and heat the entire ring until it turns a rosy hue. Continue heating the ring until the solder flows into the join, and immediately remove the heat. Use copper tongs to place the soldered ring in the pickle solution and then in plain water to rinse it. Dry the ring when you finish rinsing it. Repeat with the rest of the rings.

Shape the links. After the rings have been soldered, they need to be shaped into ovals. Put a ring over the tips of a roundnose pliers. Gently pull the ring into an oval by opening the jaws of the pliers **[3]**. Remove the oval and use the pliers to pinch the center across the narrow width to give the oval an hourglass shape **[4]**. Place the narrow section of the link over one jaw of the pliers and press the link around the jaw of the pliers **[5]**. To assure consistency in sizing subsequent links, use a pen to mark the jaw where you formed the link. Shape the rest of the links.

Connect the links. Join the links to each other by feeding one looped end of one link through both looped ends of another link **[6]**. Rotate the links until they nestle together **[7]**. Continue joining links until you are about 1 inch (2.5cm) short of the bracelet's finished length.

Fine-tune the links. At this stage of the process, the connected links have four distinct sides. Making each side of a link symmetrical also makes the links similar in size. Clamp a small round mandrel in a bench vise with the tapered end pointing up. Gently slide one side of the link over the mandrel as far as you can without distorting it or the links connected to it. Remove the link, rotate it to the next side, and slide it to the same point on the mandrel **[8]**. Repeat with the last two sides of the link. Do this with all the links.

To make the links more regular in shape and less square, clamp the wood draw plate in the bench vise. Select a hole in the plate that is slightly smaller than most of the links. Use a short length of wire to thread the chain through the hole in the plate. Using tongs or pliers, pull the chain through the hole **[9]**. Continue pulling the

chain through progressively smaller holes until the links are attractively rounded.

Use small round and half-round jeweler's files to remove any marks on the links. Then sand the spots with 300-grit sandpaper.

Add a clasp. Use 18-gauge wire and a 6mm rod to make two more jump rings. Join one ring to each end of the clasp, and use super-easy solder to solder them closed. Attach an S-hook clasp to one of the rings.

Polish the bracelet. Rub the links of the bracelet with steel wool or a brass brush – or, for more shine, polish it in a tumbler with burnishing compound and stainless steel shot. To avoid injury, do not use a machine with a rotating wheel or buff to polish the chain while you hold it.

materials
- sterling silver wire:
  - 10 feet (3m) 20-gauge round, dead-soft
  - 3 inches (7.6cm) 18-gauge round dead-soft
- 3–4 inches (7.6–10.2cm) scrap wire
- S-hook clasp

tools and supplies
- saw blades, size 5/0
- 300-grit sandpaper
- ½-inch (13mm) diameter rod or dowel
- roundnose pliers
- bench vise and pin
- jeweler's saw frame
- 2 pairs chainnose pliers
- metal snips
- soldering station: handheld butane torch, easy and super-easy solder, charcoal block, pickle pot with pickle, flux, cross-locking tweezers, soldering pick, small paintbrush, copper tongs
- drying cloth
- fine-tip marking pen
- small mandrel
- wood draw plate
- draw tongs or pliers
- small round and half-round jeweler's files
- 6mm-8-inch (20.3cm) rod or dowel
- steel wool or brass brush
- tumbler with stainless steel shot and burnishing compound (optional)

Put a little
spring
in your
links

Two quick bends is all it takes to transform a wire coil into a spring link.

by Vicki Walker

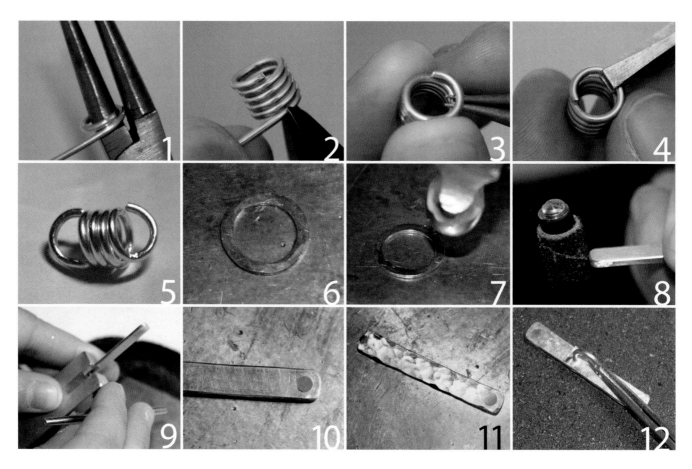

This coiled and looped necklace combines a sampling of basic wire- and metalworking skills – including forging, soldering, and riveting – that will give you the freedom to create your own chain patterns. Experiment with different-sized links in your necklace, and repetition will become a design element that is anything but predictable.

Make the springs. Work directly from a 10-foot (3m) spool or coil of 18-gauge sterling silver wire. Use flush cutters to trim the end of the wire. Grip the end of the wire in long roundnose pliers at the base of the jaw. Wrap the wire around the jaw **[1]**. Continue wrapping the wire around the pliers, making each wrap in the same location on the jaw so that all the wraps have the same inside diameter (you could also use a mandrel for this step). Make five complete revolutions, and then cut the wire **[2]**. Make a total of eight springs.

Make the spring links. Spread the top coil away from the rest of the spring with roundnose pliers **[3]**. Insert flatnose pliers in place of the roundnose pliers **[4]**. Holding the spring in one hand, use the flatnose pliers to make a 90-degree bend

in the end coil, creating a half-loop that is perpendicular to the spring. Repeat on the other end of the spring to make another half-loop **[5]**. Make half-loops on the ends of the other seven springs.

Flatten and texturize nine 14-gauge jump rings. Use a chasing hammer to flatten nine 14-gauge (1.6mm) 12.7mm inner-diameter soldered jump rings **[6]**.

Use the rounded end of the chasing hammer to hammer a dimpled texture on one side of each jump ring **[7]**. Repeat on the other side of each jump ring.

Cut and smooth a piece of flat wire to make a bar. Cut a 1¼-inch (32mm) piece of 1.5 x 5mm flat wire. Using a flex shaft or Dremel tool with a sandpaper cylinder, round and smooth the ends of the wire **[8]**.

You could also use files to shape the edges, but it will take longer.

Add rivets and texture to the bar. Use a screw-action punch or a drill to make a 1.6mm hole ⅛ inch (3mm) from each end of the bar **[9]**. Place a ⅛-inch (3mm) piece of 14-gauge copper wire in one hole. Flare the end of the copper wire with the ball-peen end of the chasing hammer. Turn the bar over to hammer the other end of the wire, making a decorative rivet. Make another decorative rivet at the other end of the bar **[10]**. Using the ball-peen end of the hammer, hammer a dimpled texture on both sides of the bar **[11]**.

- sterling silver wire:
  - 2 feet (61.0cm) 18-gauge, round, dead-soft
  - 6½ feet (2m) 16-gauge, round, dead-soft (optional)
  - 1¼ inches (32mm) flat (1.5 x 5mm)
- 1 inch (25.5mm) 14-gauge, round, half-hard copper wire
- sterling silver jump rings:
  - 9 12.7mm inside diameter (ID), 14-gauge, soldered
  - 103 5mm ID 16-gauge

tools and supplies
- flush cutters
- chainnose pliers
- flatnose pliers
- roundnose pliers
- chasing hammer

- bench block or anvil
- 5mm wooden dowels (optional)
- bench pin (optional)
- jeweler's saw, 2/0 blades (optional)
- soldering station: handheld butane torch, easy solder, charcoal block, pickle pot with pickle, flux, cross-locking tweezers, soldering pick
- flex shaft or Dremel tool, sandpaper cylinder (optional)
- screw-action punch or 1.6mm drill bit
- hand files
- sandpaper, various grits
- finishing items (choose from): polishing cloth, liver of sulfur, tumbler with stainless steel shot and burnishing compound

13

Add a connecting loop to make the toggle bar. Cut one 16-gauge, 5mm-inside-diameter jump ring in half. File and sand the cut ends of the jump ring, and make sure that the cut ends are flush with the back of the bar **[12]**. Flux the bar and the jump ring, and use easy solder to solder the cut ends of the jump ring to the back of the bar. Pickle, rinse, and dry the toggle bar.

Make the chain. Using 16-gauge jump rings, construct a 2+2+2 chain, which is a simple sequence of pairs of jump rings.

To begin the chain pattern, connect the 2+2+2 sequence to one hammered jump ring. Connect a spring link to the 2+2+2 sequence. Connect another 2+2+2 sequence to the spring link **[13]**. Repeat this pattern to the end of the chain, ending with a hammered jump ring.

Attach the toggle bar. Connect a 2+2+2 sequence to the hammered jump ring at the end of the chain. Attach the toggle bar to the 2+2+2 sequence. Finish and polish the necklace as desired.

Cascading carnelian

Create the tiered appearance of chandelier crystals in this elegant set.

by Jennifer Jordan Park

Jewelry designers are especially receptive to color, shape, and texture. In a sea of gems, an artist will fish for the ones that draw his or her attention. Displayed like ripe fruit hanging from branches, the punchy citrus color and plump pear shape of these carnelian beads made them an irresistible inspiration for the delicate chandelier-frame design of these earrings. The pattern is repeated in the bracelet, with carnelian beads and thin silver wire connecting the elements.

The wire frames are shaped and soldered together, and handmade silver balls are precisely placed to add ornate detail to the set. The finishing touches include suspending carnelian beads from the frames with wrapped loops and attaching a matching, handmade clasp to the bracelet.

Editor's Note: The designer used metric measurements when creating this set. To maintain accuracy, we chose not to include conversions in English units.

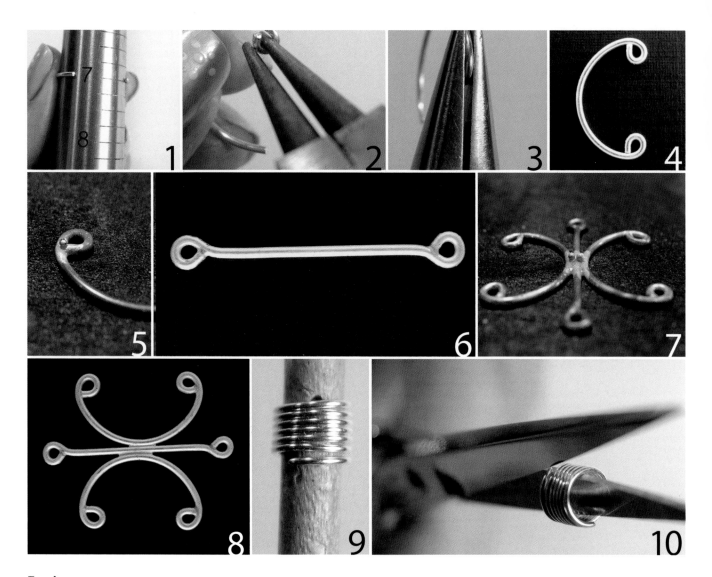

Earrings

Make four C-shaped wires. Cut a 4.2cm piece of 18-gauge wire and file the ends flat. It helps to begin with a perfectly straight piece of wire (see "Straighten It Out," p. 107.)

Form the wire into a C shape on a ring mandrel at the size 7 mark **[1]**. Grasp the C-shaped wire with your fingers about 1cm from one end, and make an inward loop at the other end using roundnose pliers **[2]**. (Holding the wire will prevent you from distorting the shape.) Repeat at the other end. (For tips on making attractive loops, see "Flawless Loops," p. 106.)

Solder the loops closed. Use chainnose pliers to adjust the loops so the C shape lies as flat as possible on a charcoal block **[3, 4]**. With a paintbrush or dropper, apply liquid flux to the areas to be joined. Heat the areas with a torch until the flux begins

to melt. (It should look clear, not white and puffy.)

Cut two tiny pallions of hard solder. Heat them on a charcoal block until they form into balls. Use a soldering pick to place them at the joins, adhering them with a tiny bit of paste flux **[5]**. Heat the solder until it flows. Use the soldering pick to nudge the solder into place if it moves during heating. Use copper tongs to place the piece in a pickle solution after soldering. Create three more C shapes. Place the subsequent ones on top of the first one to check that they are the same shape. If necessary, use your fingers or pliers to adjust them.

Make two stems. Cut a 3.7cm piece of 18-gauge wire. File the ends flat and make sure the wire is straight.

Make centered loops at each end of the wire. The ends of the loops should touch the stem. Flux both loops and solder them

closed with hard solder **[6]**. Repeat this step to make another stem.

Solder the earring frame together. On a charcoal block, arrange two C shapes on either side of one stem. Flux the areas to be soldered. Cut two pallions of medium solder, and heat them on a charcoal block until they form into balls. Place the solder at the joins where the C shapes meet the stem, adhering them with a tiny bit of paste flux **[7]**. Heat the area with a torch until the solder flows between the stem and both C shapes **[8]**. Solder the second earring frame together. Pickle both frames.

Make the silver balls. Wrap 26-gauge fine-silver wire around a ⅛-inch (3mm)-diameter dowel to form a spring **[9]**. Carefully remove the spring from the dowel. Insert one end of a pair of small metal snips into the spring and cut

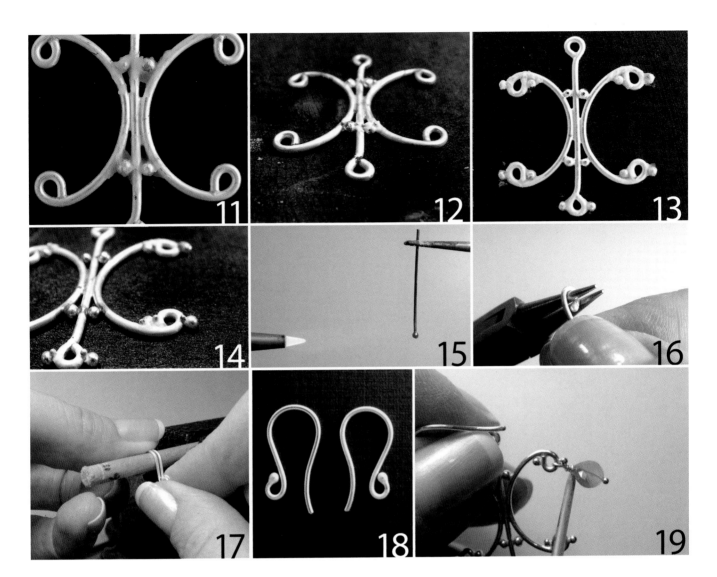

lengthwise **[10]** to produce several circular pieces of wire. Heat these individually on a charcoal block until they form into balls. Make a total of 28 silver balls.

You may need to make a few slightly larger silver balls to fit some larger spaces. To do this, lay a small snippet of silver wire so it is touching one of the balls on the charcoal block. Apply heat until the snippet is absorbed into the ball.

Solder silver balls to the stem. Place four silver balls above and below the junctions where the stem meets the C shapes. Use paste flux to "glue" them in place **[11]**. Heat until the flux is melted.

Ball up 12 tiny pallions of easy solder. Use paste flux to paste the solder balls at the joins on either side of the silver balls **[12]**. Heat until the solder flows and the balls are secured.

Solder silver balls to the loops of the C shapes. Using paste flux, adhere eight fine-silver balls to each C shape, one on the outside and one on the inside of each loop **[13]**. Also "glue" two balls to either side of the stem's bottom loop.

Create 16 tiny easy-solder balls. Use paste flux to stick the solder balls to the joins between the silver balls and the loops. Make sure there is solder where each ball touches the wire **[14]**.

Heat each area until the solder flows. Use a soldering pick to reposition the solder or the silver balls if they move. Solder the remaining balls to the second earring frame. Pickle both frames.

Make the ear wires. Cut two 5cm pieces of 20-gauge wire. Place one wire vertically in a third hand, and heat the bottom end of the wire until a small ball forms **[15]**. Repeat for the other wire. Pickle both wires.

Using roundnose pliers, make a loop at the balled end of the wire **[16]**. Repeat for the other wire.

Place a ¼-inch (6.5mm)-diameter dowel horizontally in a bench vise. With your fingers, hold the looped ends of both wires together and bend them over the dowel **[17]**. If desired, turn the wires over and bend the tail ends slightly in the opposite direction. Trim the tails to your desired length, and file the ends until smooth **[18]**.

Polish. Tumble the pieces in a rotary or vibratory tumbler to work-harden and polish them. Polish all components using a buffing wheel with tripoli and rouge.

Attach the beads. Cut ten 3.5cm pieces of 26-gauge fine-silver wire. Place one wire vertically in a third hand, and heat the bottom end until a ball forms. Repeat for the other nine pieces, and string one

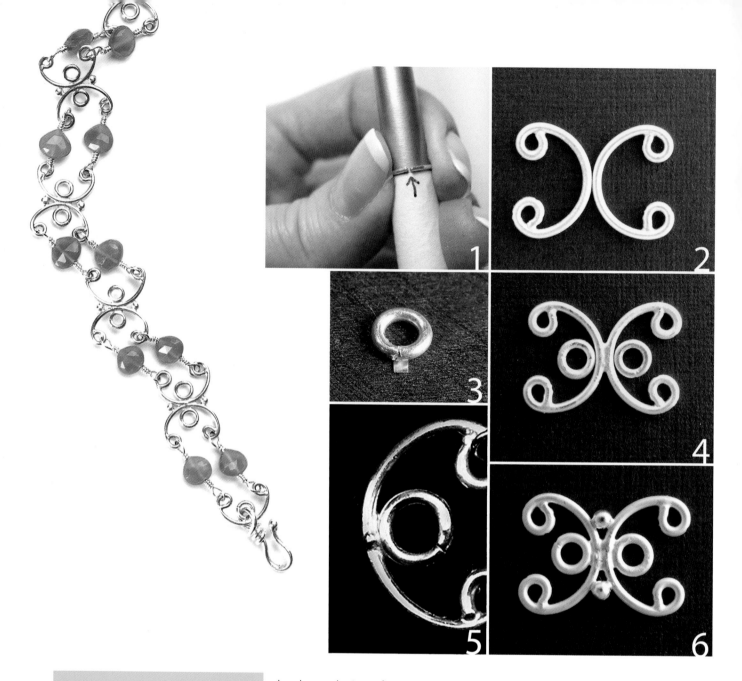

flawless
loops

To get a tight, perfectly rolled loop, use chainnose pliers to pull the loop out to the side slightly, as if you were opening a jump ring. Insert roundnose pliers into the loop, and roll it slightly to tighten it. Use the chainnose pliers to push the loop back into position, as though you were closing a jump ring.

bead on each piece of wire. Attach the beaded dangles to each frame loop with wrapped loops. Make sure the wrapped loops are not large enough to slide over the silver balls on the frame [19].

Attach ear wires. Using chainnose pliers, open the balled end of the ear wire. Slide the top loop of the frame stem onto the open ear wire. Close the balled end of the ear wire. Repeat for the other earring.

Bracelet

Make the C shapes. For a 7-inch (17.8cm) bracelet, cut 14 2.8cm pieces of 20-gauge sterling silver wire. For an 8-inch (20.3cm) bracelet, cut 16 pieces. File the ends flat.

Wrap tape around a bezel mandrel at the 8.5mm-diameter location [1]. Form the wires into C shapes by bending them over the mandrel at the taped location. Using roundnose pliers, make small loops at the ends of each C shape, and solder the loops closed with hard solder, as in the earrings.

Solder the C shapes together to form links. To make one link, place two C shapes on a charcoal block with their backs touching [2]. Solder them together using one piece of balled-up hard solder.

Make a total of six links. The remaining two individual C shapes will be used for the clasp pieces.

Make 14 jump rings. Use 20-gauge sterling silver wire and a 5/64-inch (2mm) dowel and saw or flush cutters to make 14 jump rings. The inner diameter should be about 2mm, the outer diameter should be about 3.5mm. Close the rings tightly.

Solder the rings closed. Cut a tiny pallion of hard solder, and place it on a charcoal block. Place a closed ring on top of the solder, making sure the area of the ring to be joined sits directly on the solder [3]. Apply liquid flux to the join. Heat the ring until the solder flows into the join. Solder all rings, then pickle and rinse them.

Solder the rings to the links and clasp pieces. Using medium solder, solder two rings to each of the six links, one to the left of center and one to the right [4]. Also solder a ring to the inner curve of each C-shaped clasp piece [5]. Pickle and rinse.

Solder silver balls to each link's joins. Make 12 silver balls, as in the earrings, except use 26-gauge fine silver wire on a ³⁄₁₆-inch (5mm)-diameter dowel. On each of the six links, place the balls at the top and bottom joins where the two C shapes meet [6]. Solder the balls in place using easy solder.

Polish. Tumble the pieces in a rotary or vibratory tumbler to work-harden them. Polish all components on a buffing wheel with tripoli and rouge.

Assemble the links. Attach a piece of 26-gauge sterling silver wire to a link's loop with a wrapped loop. String a 5.5 x 5.5mm center-drilled carnelian bead, and use a second wrapped loop to connect the wire to the corresponding loop on a second link. Repeat until all the links are connected by both loops, with the clasps parts on each end [7].

Make a hook and attach it to one clasp piece. Cut a 7cm piece of 18-gauge sterling silver wire. Heat one end of the wire to form a ball. Pickle and rinse the wire.

With roundnose pliers, bend the balled end into a hook. Attach the hook to one clasp piece with a wrapped loop. Trim any excess, and file if necessary [8].

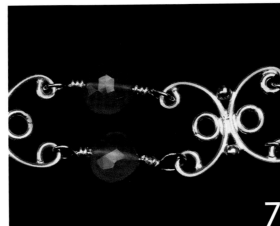
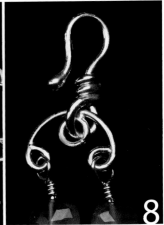

materials

- sterling silver wire:
  - 10¾ inches (27cm) 18-gauge round, dead-soft
  - 25½ inches (65cm) 20-gauge round, dead-soft
  - 27½ inches (70cm) 26-gauge round, half-hard
- 28¾ inches (73cm) 26-gauge fine-silver wire, round, dead-soft
- 24 5.5mm beads

tools and supplies

- flush cutters
- flat file
- 2 steel blocks (optional)
- ring mandrel
- chainnose pliers
- roundnose pliers
- soldering station: torch with small or medium tip; charcoal block; small paintbrush or dropper; liquid flux; hard, medium, and easy solder; soldering pick; paste flux; copper tongs; pickle pot with pickle
- jewelry scissors
- dowels: ⅛-inch (3.2mm), ¼-inch (6.4mm), ³⁄₁₆-inch (4.8mm) diameters
- third hand
- bench vise
- tumbler, rotary or vibratory
- polishing compounds, red rouge and/or tripoli
- buffing wheel
- magnifiers (optional)

straighten
it out

To straighten a curved piece of wire, roll it between two steel blocks. This will work-harden it, so you may need to anneal it when you're finished.

Contributors

Linda Augsburg has been making jewelry since 1998 when the Bead Hawk bead shop opened next door to the quilt shop she managed in Jacksonville Beach, Fla. She has worked on all three of Kalmbach's jewelry titles and many special issues. She can be contacted in care of Kalmbach Books.

Connie Fox is inspired by eagles. Eagles have the capacity to soar to the heavens and bring back to earth the energy, light, and wisdom of the upper worlds. It is this energy that she strives to bring to her jewelry designs and to her classes. She may be contacted through her Web site, conniefox.com.

Leslee Frumin started taking art and craft classes as a child in Michigan, and is now a bead and metal artist in San Juan Capistrano, California. She teaches metal, jewelry, and off-loom beadweaving techniques. Visit her Web site at lesleefrumin.com to see more of her creations or contact her via e-mail at lesfrumin@aol.com, or by phone at (949) 456-0718.

Lisa Niven Kelly has been teaching beadwork and wirework for over 15 years. Currently, her work focuses on wirework, incorporating beads whenever possible. These days you'll find her sticking close to home with her two young daughters and managing her new Web site, beaducation.com, which hosts online beadwork and wirework classes. Contact her via e-mail at info@lisanivenkelly.com.

Anna Lemons' motto is "When life hands you lemons, make jewelry!" You can learn more about Anna and her jewelry on her Web site, annalemonsjewelry.com.

Julia Lowther has been teaching jewelry making nationally and internationally for almost a decade. Her current work focuses on reviving and expanding the ancient art of chain making. She loves the process of transforming stiff, unruly coils of wire into delightfully flexible and sensuous ribbons of chain. She lives and works in Seattle, Wash.

Anne Mitchell currently resides in Tucson, Ariz. She is a full-time designer, instructor, and author, specializing in chain making and metalworking. Visit her Web site, annemitchell.net.

Angel Ortiz learned to make wire jewelry from his wife, **Joanne Ortiz,** who's been making jewelry for ten years. Together they own PurpleLily Designs, which not only features beaded and wire jewelry, but also Joanne's handcrafted lampworked and polymer clay beads. Visit their Web site at purplelilydesigns.com.

Jennifer Jordan Park, a native Southerner, has a background in graphic design and now devotes most of her time to creating jewelry. She enjoys working with different colors, forms, and shapes of metal, gemstones, and glass. Visit her Web site, weareverjewelry.com, to see her latest designs.

Karen Rakoski finds inspiration for her designs in nature. Her jewelry pieces are influenced by her engineering background and the other crafts she's explored, which range from lace making to knife making. She's usually busy teaching at Studio 34 in Rochester, and thinking of new designs. Contact her via e-mail at knrak@rochester.rr.com

Kate Ferrant Richbourg has been making jewelry for more than 15 years and is co-owner of Beadissimo in San Francisco. Visit her Web site at beadissimo.com.

Amy Robleski was the editorial assistant for *Art Jewelry* when the magazine began as a bimonthly publication. Though she has since moved to her husband's hometown, she continues to keep her finger on the pulse of the craft world. She appreciates crafting because it gives her time to reflect while creating something from scratch. Contact her via e-mail at amyrobleski@yahoo.com.

Kriss Silva has been teaching jewelry workshops from Hawaii to Milwaukee since 1996, and currently lives on the North Shore of Oahu. She enjoys inspiring her students to achieve individual expression and share ideas and inspiration. She is currently the class coordinator for Bead It in Honolulu, Hawaii, and can be reached via e-mail at krisssilva@yahoo.com.

Gretta Van Someren loves to create jewelry that reflects the unique personalities and moods of the wearer. She owns Attérg Jewelry Design. Visit her Web site, atterg.com.

Vicki Walker has been making jewelry for over eight years and enjoys trying new techniques. She loves creating beautiful things, and especially enjoys incorporating lampwork beads into her jewelry. Her jewelry can be seen on her Web site, wiremania.com.

Wendy Witchner is a wire and metal artist who lives in her motor home and constantly travels the United States, selling her creations at shows nationwide. Visit her Web site, wendywitchner-jewelry.com.

Kristi Zevenbergen teaches beading, wireworking, and metalsmithing in the Seattle area. She loves helping others discover the joy and freedom of creating. You can see more of her work on her Web site, kristizevenbergen.com. Contact her via e-mail at kristiskitsch@comcast.net.

Resources

Many jewelry-making supplies can be purchased from your local craft, hardware, jewelry, and bead stores. The resources listed below supplied many of the tools and materials used for the projects in this book.

Allcraft Jewelry Suppy: 800.645.7124, allcraftonline.com

Contenti: 800.343.3364, contenti.com

Euro Tool: 800.552.3131, eurotool.com

Fire Mountain Gems: 800.355.2137, firemountaingems.com

G&S Metals: 800.852.3860, gsgold.com

Harbor Freight Tools: 805.388.3000, harborfreight.com

Hauser and Miller: 800.462.7447, hauserandmiller.com

Hoover and Strong: 800.759.9997, hooverandstrong.com

Lindstrom Tools: lindstromtools.com

Metalliferous: 888.944.0909, metalliferous.com

Online Metals: 800.704.2157, onlinemetals.com

Otto Frei: 800.772.3456, ottofrei.com

Rio Grande: 800.545.6566, riogrande.com

Thunderbird Supply Company: 800.545.7968, thunderbirdsupply.com

Also, be sure to check national and regional craft chain stores in your area for tools and materials.

Glossary

ALLOY A mixture of two or more metallic elements.

ANNEALING Heating work-hardened metal to restore malleability.

BENCH PIN A work surface extension with a V-shaped notch, used to provide support for jewelry-making tasks.

BENCH VISE A clamp used to secure items to a workbench.

BEZEL A strip of flat wire that surrounds and secures a stone or other object; can also be made of several separate wires.

CHASING Using a hammer and steel tools to recess and/or reshape metal from the front.

FIRESCALE A surface layer of cupric oxide that forms when copper-bearing alloys are heated.

FLUX Chemicals that prevent oxides from forming when metal is heated.

FORGING The process of shaping metal with the help of heat and/or hammers.

GAUGE A unit of measure describing the thickness of wire or metal; a tool used in measurement.

LIVER OF SULFUR Potassium sulfide; dissolved in water to create a patina on metal.

OXIDATION Metal becoming tarnished or darkened by exposure to oxygen or by the use of chemicals.

PALLION Small snippet of sheet solder.

PATINA Surface film created on metal for a colored or darkened finish; often used to make texture stand out.

PICKLE A chemical solution that removes flux residue and oxides from metal; also, to dip something in pickle.

PIERCING Using a jeweler's saw to cut shapes from the interior of a sheet of metal.

PIN VISE A clamp designed to twist shut around a narrow form, such as wire.

PLANISH The process of smoothing, flattening, and work-hardening metal by hammering.

POLISH (also BURNISH, TUMBLE) To refine the surface of metal, making it smooth and shiny.

POLISHING CLOTH A soft cloth that is precharged with polishing compounds such as tripoli or red rouge.

QUENCH To quickly cool hot metal in liquid.

RIVET To fasten or decorate a surface by inserting a pin into a premade hole and flaring each end of the pin to hold it in place.

SOLDER A lower-melting-point alloy of the same metal as the workpiece; when heated, solder flows into the spaces between two pieces of metal, forming a bond.

TEMPER (also MALLEABILITY) The hardness of wire and metal. Jewelry-making wire comes in three tempers: hard, half-hard, and dead-soft.

Bending or tumbling metal will work-harden it, making it less malleable.

THIRD HAND Clamping pliers often used to hold pieces during soldering.

TORCH An open-flame heat source that can produce temperatures higher than the melting point of the metal being used. Simple one-part torches use compressed gas and atmospheric oxygen; more complex torches combine compressed gas and compressed oxygen to reach higher temperatures.

TRUE-UP To perfect a shape to the commonly perceived ideal form of that shape, whether it is a circle, square, oval, or other shape.

WORK-HARDEN To make metal less malleable by altering it. Work processes such as twisting, shaping, and hammering can be used to alter the temper of metal.

Index

Jewelry-making resources for all Metal Clay skill levels!

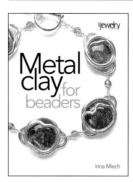
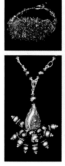
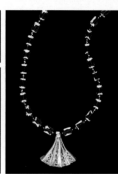

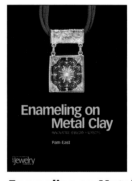
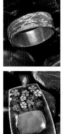